Living with a
Pug

Edited by Alison Mount

BARRON'S

THE QUESTION OF GENDER
The "he" pronoun is used throughout this book in favor of the rather impersonal "it," but no gender bias is intended at all.

ACKNOWLEDGMENTS
The publisher would like to thank the following for help with photography: Pat Withers (Witherford), Diane Timmis (Dachsvale), Jeff and Anne Phillips (Jansclan), and Doreen Davies (Poosbury).

First edition for the United States and Canada published in 2003 by Barron's Educational Series, Inc.

All inquiries should be addressed to:

Barron's Educational Series, Inc.
250 Wireless Boulevard
Hauppauge, NY 11788
http://www.barronseduc.com

International Standard Book Number 0-7641-5635-7

Library of Congress Catalog Card Number 20021110449

PRINTED IN SINGAPORE
9 8 7 6 5 4 3 2

CONTENTS

CHAPTER ONE

INTRODUCING THE PUG

There is no other breed like the Pug. Not only does he look distinctive, but he has a character like no other. His furrowed brow may make him appear perpetually worried, but beneath the wrinkles lies a happy-go-lucky dog with a clownlike personality.

Ask Pug owners to describe their dogs, and the same words crop up time and again: "loving," "intelligent," "alert," and "inquisitive." However, one word appears more than any other – "fun!" This is a dog that will keep you amused for hours with his antics, and who will thrive on your smiles and laughter.

Once you have shared your home and your life with one of these unique dogs, you will understand the breed motto: *Multum in parvo* – a lot of dog in a small space!

IMPERIAL HERITAGE

In common with many Toy dogs, the Pug is thought to derive from China. An ancient breed, he dates back to around 400 B.C.E., although exact details cannot be verified because records were destroyed by Emperor Ch'in Shih in 225 B.C.E.

Certainly, we know that a dog very similar to today's Pug was sent as a diplomatic gift from Korea to Japan in A.D. 732. These tributes were important in maintaining foreign relations, and were generally expensive or exotic in tone. Clearly, the Pug-type – or Ssuchuan Pai dog, as it was called – was highly regarded in the Chinese court.

The word "Ssuchuan" refers to the Chinese province that the dog may have derived from, and the word "pai" describes the dog as being short-faced and short-legged – pets that could fit easily underneath the low Chinese dining tables.

Two centuries later, the Ssuchuan Pai had become known as Lo-chiang, Lo-chiang-sze, and Lo-sze (after the Ssuchuan town). In the Shandong province of China, lapdogs called Ha-pa were highly esteemed. Some were short-coated (Pug types), others were long-coated (Peke and Shih Tzu types).

SELECTIVE BREEDING
The Shih Tzu (below), the Pekingese (below left), and the Pug (below right)
were interbred to produce small, flat-faced dogs.

The breed grew in popularity up to the time of the Ming Dynasty (1368–1644), when the cat found favor and ousted the Pug and his Toy cousins from the royal court. By the end of the 17th century, however, the Lo-sze regained its popularity, together with the Pekingese and the Shih Tzu.

There is likely to have been some amount of interbreeding between these three dogs at some point – to achieve the flat faces, or, in the case of the Shih Tzu and Peke, to improve their coats.

It was once believed that the dogs' flat faces were achieved through physical brutality – that the Pug had its nose bones deliberately crushed to shorten the muzzle – but this is untrue. Such actions would only affect the dog whose nose had been broken – the offspring would have been normal.

In fact, the flat face was achieved through selective breeding – simply put, this would have involved choosing dogs that naturally had shorter muzzles than other dogs, and breeding them together. Over a period of time and with good matchmaking, the muzzle would gradually shorten further.

Chinese breeders were particularly keen on coat patterns and other symbols. In the Pug's case, they deemed the forehead wrinkle formation especially important, and bred to produce a W-shaped wrinkle – the Chinese symbol for "prince."

THE DOWAGER EMPRESS

One person who was opposed to interbreeding between the Pug, Peke, and Shih Tzu was the Dowager Empress Tzu Hsi. An autocratic, cunning woman, she effectively ruled China for the latter half of the 19th century.

A great dog lover, the Empress's main passion was the Pekingese, but she also owned Pugs and Shih Tzus. All the palace dogs were treated like kings, and were fed a diet of shark fins, curlew livers, quail breast, and antelope milk!

MASTIFF MADNESS

The Pug has vague similarities to the Mastiff, which led early canine historians to believe that the two are directly related. At one time in England, the Pug was called the Dutch Mastiff because of this belief.

However, the Pug is not a miniature Mastiff – the skull shapes are entirely different, and the two breeds' histories are quite distinct.

The distinctive Mastiff markings include the ears, the muzzle, the nose, and around the eyes.
Photo: Anne-Marie Class

The Pug has many simian qualities. Character-wise, he is playful, clownish, and a little mischievous. Perhaps this is why the breed is called "Pug" – an old English nickname for a monkey or dog (often used as a term of endearment for naughty children).

Another theory is completely unconnected to other animals – that the word "Pug" comes from the Latin meaning "clenched fist," as in pugilist (boxer).

It is easy to detect the Pug's monkeylike qualities.

When she died in 1908, palace eunuchs continued breeding the Empress's dogs, but the methods – and results – were haphazard, lacking all the planning and skill for which the Empress was famed.

PALACE POOCHES

The revered Toy breeds (particularly the Shih Tzu, Pekingese, and Pug) were considered precious animals, and were not seen outside the Imperial Palace in Peking (now Beijing). The dogs became synonymous with royalty and so ordinary citizens were forbidden to own them – disobeying this rule was sometimes punishable by death.

Some dogs did manage to escape the palace walls, however. Eunuchs entrusted with the dogs' care are thought to have smuggled out substandard specimens that would not be used for breeding, and sold them to the highest bidder.

EUROPEAN TREASURES

Several dogs ended up in the hands of European traders. In the early 16th century, Portugal, shortly followed by Spain, Holland, and England, was trading with China, and the exotic Chinese dogs were highly treasured.

Once in Europe, Pugs, together with other Chinese Toy breeds, retained their aristocratic links, and became the companions of royalty all over Europe.

Emperor K'anf Hsi gave Pugs as gifts to Peter the Great of Russia (1672–1725), and the maiden aunt of Catherine the Great (1729–1796) was a devoted lover of the breed. Reputed to have kept 16 in her bedroom, she hired a maid whose sole duty was to look after her little darlings.

THE DUTCH DOG

Dutch traders took the Pug to Holland, where he thrived, thanks to a little Pug called Pompey.

Pompey accompanied his owner, William the Silent (1533–1584), everywhere. When on a campaign against the Spanish, William, Prince of Orange, camped at Hermigny, in France. During a surprise night attack by the Spanish, Pompey saved his master's life by alerting him to the approach of the enemy.

According to Sir Roger Williams's *Actions of the Lowe Countries* of 1618:

The Pug was quick to find favor in Holland.

NOT TONIGHT, JOSEPHINE

Napoleon's beloved, Josephine, was a devoted Pug owner, and the proud owner of Fortuné. When imprisoned at Les Carmes, Josephine hid secret messages under the dog's collar, which he took to Napoleon.

Things didn't go quite as smoothly on the couple's wedding night, however. Fortuné decided to sleep on the bed, and was prepared to defend this right – to the point of taking a chunk out of Napoleon's leg when he approached the bed!

"…the dogge, hearing a great noyse, fell to scratching and crying and withall leapt on the Prince's face, awaking him being asleep, before any of his men. And albeit the Prince lay in his armes, with a lackey alwaies holding on his horses ready bridled. Yet, at the going out of his tent, with much adoe he recovered his horse before the enemie arrived."

Although there were casualties in the Dutch camp, the Prince was not among them. Pompey became a national hero because of his actions, and was adopted as the mascot for the House of Orange. Sir Roger writes:

"Ever since, to the Prince's dying day, he kept one of the dog's race, and so did many of his friendes and followers."

Even in death, Williams is united with his favorite breed. On his tomb in Delft Cathedral, Holland, a Pug is carved at the feet of Williams's effigy.

The British royal family adopted the Pug as a special favorite.

BRITISH ROYALTY

It was through the Pug's Dutch links that the breed was introduced to Britain. When William and Mary took the British throne in 1688, their Pugs joined them, decorated with orange ribbons.

Pugs remained in the royal house for several centuries. Queen Victoria, renowned for her love of dogs, had several Pugs, many from the top breeders of the day. She kept careful records of her dogs – their dates of birth, parentage, etc. – in a book entitled *Dogs in the Home Park Kennel at Windsor.* Those mentioned in the book include Duchess, Fatima, Mops, Olga, and Topsy. Bosco was said to be a favorite in the royal household, and is buried in the gardens of Frogmore House, Windsor.

During Victorian times, Pugs often had their ears cropped. However, Queen Victoria preferred dogs to look as nature intended, and all her dogs had their ears intact. Other breed enthusiasts soon followed suit.

When the Queen died in 1901, her son, Edward VII, succeeded her, and Pugs continued to be an important part of royal family life – Victoria's children having inherited their mother's love of the breed.

Edward VIII, Duke of Windsor, who abdicated in order to marry Wallis Simpson, was a great fan of the Pug, and he and his wife even exhibited their dogs in France, the country they took refuge in. The Duchess is said to have treated her Pugs as substitute children, dressing them in mink collars, feeding them haute cuisine, and even spraying them daily with Christian Dior perfume!

The Duke's favorite dog, Diamond, was with him when he died, and pined terribly afterwards. The dog refused to eat, and his health deteriorated. Diamond died within a matter of weeks of his master. It was reported in the national newspapers that the devoted little dog had died of a broken heart.

THE LADY'S COMPANION

The Pug's royal links made him popular with the aristocracy, who were eager to surround themselves with the same possessions as those they aspired to. Decorated in ribbons to match his mistress's dress, the Pug took his place in grand homes across Britain, particularly in the Victorian and Edwardian eras.

The craze for very small Toy breeds also took hold. According to the satirical magazine *Punch*:

"The cult of the Toy dog has reached a stage where ladies have to look at the little darlings through a microscope."

BREED DEVELOPMENT

The Pug owes a great debt of gratitude to two kennels from the mid-1800s, who established

---

WHAT'S IN A NAME?

In the English language, the Pug has the shortest name of any dog breed, but throughout its history, the breed has been known by many different names around the world.

Finland	Mopsi
France	Carlin
Germany	Mops Hund
Holland	Mops Hond
Italy	Carlino
Spain	Doguillo
Sweden	Mops

The "Mops" name derives from the Dutch word, meaning "to mope" – clearly referring to the breed's unhappy-looking expression. In contrast, the "Carlin/Carlino" name refers to Carlin, a French actor who played a harlequin clown in the 18th century. Clearly, early breed enthusiasts looked beneath the Pug's frown to appreciate the clownlike character inside.

---

the breed in the UK (from this foundation, dogs were exported to America).

Lord and Lady Willoughby d'Eresby from Lincolnshire imported some dogs from Russia and Austria, and produced dark fawn and black Pugs. London breeder, Charlie Morrison, bred light-colored apricot Pugs, and had stock from Holland. Even today, Pugs can be described as Willoughby or Morrison dogs, according to their color and type. Once established, the two lines used each other's stock, occasionally importing dogs from Europe to add fresh blood.

The Pug Dog Club of England was established in 1881, and was formally accepted by the Kennel Club (KC) two years later (one of the first breed clubs to achieve formal KC recognition). The breed was granted Championship status in 1886, and the first Champions were: Ch. Diamond, Ch. Boffin, Ch. Second Challenger, Ch. Stingo Sniffles, and Ch. Little Gipsy Queen.

AMERICAN PUG

Around the same time, dogs began to be exported from Britain to America – often at extraordinarily high prices. In 1900, Mrs. Gould, a New York Pug fancier, paid $500 (£350) for Black Night and Canonbury Princess – exorbitant price tags for the day.

The key U.S. Pug breeder at the start of the 20th century was Al Eberhardt, from Ohio, who imported Finsbury (bred by Miss Harris) and Haughty (bred by Mrs. Houlker) from the U.K. The Haughty line was very influential in the

American fanciers were prepared to pay high prices to import the breed.

early history of the American Pug – indeed, Ch. Haughty Madge was one of the first dogs to be registered in the U.S.

Although the Pug was recognized by the American Kennel Club (AKC) as early as 1885, the first breed club was not formed until 1931, when the Pug Dog Club of America was established by East Coast breeders. The first Pug show took place six years later in 1937, held in Madison, New Jersey.

THE BLACK PUG

Another influence on the breed was British aristocrat Lady Brassey, who, in the latter half of the 19th century, travelled to far-flung reaches of the world and wrote about her experiences in her journal.

Lady Brassey often voyaged in the Far East, where she may well have encountered Pugs. She was particularly known for black Pugs, and wrote about them fondly in her diary.

Lady Brassey was not the first to introduce the color to the U.K., but she was the first to popularize it. In a class for black Pugs at the Maidstone Show, Kent, in 1886, Lady Brassey owned all the entrants! Within just a few years, the black Pug was a more frequent sight (also thanks to Queen Victoria owning a couple – one from Lady Brassey).

During the 1960s and 1970s, black Pugs became particularly popular in America and many were exported from England. Today, the fawn is more dominant in the show ring, but black Pugs still have a dedicated following, on both sides of the Atlantic.

The black Pug has an enthusiastic fan club.

LAST CHINESE DOGS

In 1949, the Chinese Communist Party came to power. The Party considered it a waste of food to keep pet dogs when its own people were starving, and ordered the destruction of all dogs.

Fortunately for the Pug, British soldiers had sacked the Imperial Palace in Peking in the 1860s, and took some Pugs and Pekingese to the U.K.

Among the treasures taken from the palace were two apricot fawn Pugs, Moss and Lamb. Said to have closely resembled each other, the dogs were slightly longer than they were tall, and were rather short-legged. Nevertheless, they were bred together, and produced Click, one of the most influential Pugs in the breed's history. Owned by James Watson, Click was a top sire, and is said to be in the pedigree of all modern Pugs.

THE POPULAR PUG

Dog showing soared in popularity during the 1880s, and this trend worked in the Pug's favor. Many of the exhibitors were women, with whom the Pug was a particular favorite – a lady's lapdog. As a result, the breed was a popular dog at shows, with high numbers of entrants in each class, and this increased the breed's profile.

The 20th century saw several peaks and valleys in the Pug's popularity. Like all breeds, the two world wars affected him badly, as dog showing and breeding came to a virtual halt. However, Pug popularity revived and is now enjoying something of an upsurge once more. In the U.K., in the last 10 years, Pug Kennel Club registrations have risen steadily from 604 in 1992 through to 871 in 2001. In the U.S., registrations are considerably higher – in 2001, the Pug ranked the 14th most popular breed, with 12,518 dogs being registered with the AKC.

Modern life favors the small dog – particularly a short-coated one. Pug owners do not need spacious homes, acres of garden, or large cars to accommodate their dogs, nor do they have to give over their free time to long walks or grooming sessions. They just need to give their pets oodles of love – and with a dog who is as much fun and as adorable as the Pug, this is not exactly a hardship!

RICH AND FAMOUS

The Pug has an adoring fan-base, and includes some very famous owners from past and present, including:

Harriet Beecher Stowe

Napoleon Bonaparte and Josephine de Beauharnais

Sir Winston Churchill

Sammy Davis, Jr.

William Hogarth

Valentino

Voltaire

Andy Warhol

Prince Rainier and Princess Grace of Monaco

Marie Antoinette

CHAPTER TWO

CHOOSING A PUG

Falling head over heels in love with the Pug is not difficult – for most people, it is impossible to resist the breed's large, dark-brown eyes and adorable, wrinkly face. Gaze into those rich, dreamy eyes and you could be lost to the breed forever.

However, although the Pug is a Toy breed, he is not a toy. He is a living creature who will share your life for the next 12 years or so. It is important that you do not make a rash decision and buy a puppy on impulse. In the cold, clear light of day, ask yourself the following questions – and be honest in your replies.

Are your work commitments suitable?

Will the dog be left for more than four hours a day? It is recommended that no dog should be left alone for a longer period than this. The Pug is an especially companionable breed and will not thrive in an environment where he is regularly left home alone for long hours.

Does your lifestyle accommodate responsible dog ownership?

As well as your work commitments, do you have the time to house-train a Pug, give him hours of companionship each day, set aside time to train and socialize him, and walk him twice-daily too? In the beginning, these things will seem like a novelty, but, when that wears off, you must be disciplined to continue to care for your Pug 24/7.

Can you cope with the mess?

If you are extremely tidy, are you sure you can cope with dog hair and muddy pawprints on your designer sofa, carpet, expensive white bed linen, or in your new car? And don't forget the inevitable accidents while the puppy is being house-trained.

Can you afford a dog?

Pugs are not cheap to buy, and are even more expensive to maintain. On top of the initial cost of buying his accessories (bed, lead and collar, food bowls, crate, etc.), there are the ongoing expenses, such as dog food, toys, boarding kennel fees, and costly veterinary bills. (See page 24.)

Are you fit enough to cope with a Pug?

A retired couple make great Pug owners – both being at home all day to provide him with the companionship that he craves – but elderly owners are not always suitable, and may be ill-prepared to cope with an energetic, mischievous Pug puppy. Even if you are fit and well now – will you still be able to care for your Pug 12 years from now?

Is your family suitable?

Just because the Pug is a Toy breed doesn't mean that he cannot make a superb family dog. The case history on page 38 shows that Pugs

The Pug can be a great family dog – as long as children are taught a sense of respect.

can make great companions for kids. However, this entirely depends on the family concerned. Are the children respectful of animals? Do you have complete control over them? If you ask them to calm down, will they?

It is unfair to expect a Pug to cope in a chaotic environment – and it could result in serious injury. Plus, if you cannot discipline your children and keep them under control, a mischievous, energetic Pug puppy will definitely run rings around you.

Is your home suitable?

Although Pugs do not need a lot of living space, and will happily adapt to living in an apartment, they do enjoy having access to a garden. With a puppy, easy access to the garden is imperative – or you will never get on top of house-training. If you do not have immediate garden access, you should seriously rethink having a puppy.

If you do have a yard, can it be made secure for a dog? (See page 25.)

FINDING A BREEDER

The first starting place for locating a breeder should be your national breed club (your kennel club will be able to give you details). Some clubs have puppy-lists, detailing all available litters; others rely on the breed club secretary's knowledge of who has what!

In addition, you can visit one of the larger Championship shows (such as Crufts in the U.K. or Westminster in the U.S.), or a regional Championship event, and take a good look at the Pugs that most appeal to you. You could then contact the dogs' breeders and ask their advice. If they don't have a litter planned, perhaps they could recommend someone with dogs of similar breeding who is expecting puppies.

PLACES TO AVOID

Do not buy a puppy from a pet store. The puppies will not be adequately socialized, and they could be harboring disease. Importantly, you will not know the conditions in which the puppy was raised, any hereditary conditions in the line, and the parents' temperaments – information that is vital for picking your ideal new companion.

The shop may stock several breeds, and the staff will never be as knowledgeable about the Pug as an experienced breeder. Will the staff be able to answer any query you may have outside shop hours, or agree to take the dog back five years hence if your circumstances change? I doubt it!

Puppy farm (puppy mill) dogs often end up in pet stores. Certainly, most reputable breeders would refuse to sell their stock to a shop. Puppy farms are, as their name suggests, places where dogs are churned out for profit. Females are bred from every season, with no regard for their health and well-being. The puppies are kept in dirty conditions, lack human contact and socialization with the outside world, and will make sickly, unhappy pets that could be fearful or bad-tempered.

Some puppy farms are literally like dog superstores, stocking many different breeds – you can just turn up, buy one, and take it home

It is essential to track down a breeder who has a reputation for producing sound dogs with good temperaments.

immediately. It is easy to avoid these places, but puppy farmers often operate in a more underhanded fashion. Often they employ dealers – people who, when the puppies are at a saleable age, will take the puppies (and sometimes the dam too) and keep them in their homes. This gives prospective buyers the impression that the puppies have been home-reared and lovingly cared for by the dealer, who is often happy to play along with the charade.

When the puppy farmers employ such cunning, underhanded tactics, it is easy to see how some people end up with unhealthy, poor-quality puppies, hefty veterinarian bills, and often heartache – usually with no legal recourse.

The only way you can be sure of getting a good-quality puppy is to go to a reputable breeder. Ask for the recommendations of knowledgeable people in the breed, and make sure you spend time doing your research.

VETTING THE BREEDER

Once you have a located a reputable breeder, recommended by the club, ask the following questions:

- How long has the breeder been involved in the breed?
- How many years have they been breeding Pugs?
- Why do they breed? To improve their line and for the good of the breed, or to make a quick buck?
- What after-sales service will they provide? It is reasonable to expect lifelong advice should you need it, and for the breeder to accept the puppy/dog back at any stage of his life should you encounter problems or your circumstances change. A caring breeder will always maintain his or her interest in, and responsibility to, the puppies for the entirety of their lives.
- Where will the puppies be raised? Avoid litters that have been kept outside in kennels – they will not have been exposed to everyday household sights and sounds (such as vacuum cleaners or the washing machine), and will have less contact with people. Do not underestimate the effect of early undersocialization – the lack of confidence can stay with a puppy for his entire life. You will give yourself a head start if you pick a home-reared puppy.
- What are the breeder's home circumstances? If you have a busy, family home, it is not ideal to have a puppy that has been raised in a quiet, sedate one. If you have cats, does the breeder have them? Finding a breeder whose home circumstances match your own will make it easier for the puppy to make the transition to your home.
- Have the litter's parents been X-rayed for hemivertebrae (a serious spinal problem in the breed – see page 126).

A good breeder will also be keen to ask a few questions of their own – they will want to ensure that their puppies go to the best homes possible. If they don't take an active interest in finding out about your home, family, and you, then be suspicious.

If they agree to your taking on one of their puppies, they will probably request a home visit. They will assess whether you – and other household members – can provide a safe, loving, stable, responsible home for the puppy.

Do not take offense if the breeder requests a home visit or interrogates you about your lifestyle and home life – they only have their dogs' best interests at heart. If anything, you should be pleased – it shows the breeder is responsible and caring.

VIEWING THE LITTER

If you are happy with the breeder's replies, arrange to view the litter. Because of the risk of infection to the puppies, you will be unlikely to visit before the litter is six weeks old. You may be asked to remove your shoes and to wash your hands before being allowed access to the puppies.

Although the breeder may have been

It is important to see the mother with her puppies.

recommended to you, do still make your own checks.

- Is the home clean and hygienic? A good rule of thumb is to ask: if the breeder cooked you a meal there, would you be happy to eat it?
- Do the breeder's dogs appear happy and healthy?
- Are the dogs friendly, or do they keep their distance from the owner and/or other people?
- How does the breeder treat the dogs?

Next, turn your attention to the litter. Pug puppies should be little bundles of fun – playful, inquisitive, friendly, and energetic. They will probably all scrabble around to be picked up, each one of them screaming "Me, me! Pick me!" in puppy language!

After endlessly playing with their littermates, or, if they have just been fed, the puppies may start to become sleepy and will all gradually fall asleep. However, if they are sleepy all the way through your visit, ask to view the litter again.

A healthy litter should exhibit the following signs:

- They should be healthily plump, but a distinct pot-belly can indicate worm infestation.
- The puppies should be similar sizes. Sometimes, you get monsters and runts in the same litter, and they can all grow up to be the same size, but this is the exception rather than the rule.
- There should be no sign of fleas or flea dirt in the coat. Part the fur to inspect.
- The puppies' bottoms should be clean.
- Their eyes should be clear (not red or

The puppies should be clean, lively, and inquisitive.

weeping), and there should be no discharge from their noses.

- The ears should be clean – head-shaking or excessive scratching at the ears can indicate mites.
- They should be breathing clearly.
- Character-wise, avoid any shy, nervous puppies. They may look super-cute, sitting on their own, looking all lost and alone, and you may be desperate to give one a good home. But it will take a lot of time, patience, and hard work to make a good pet out of such a dog. Heartbreaking though it is, this little fellow is best left to the experienced hands of an expert.

PICKING THE PUPPY

So you are satisfied that the breeder is the best you can find, and that the litter is happy and healthy. Now it's time to pick your puppy.

In many cases, the choice will be made for you. If the breeder will be keeping one of the puppies for the show ring, he or she will have the pick of the litter. From the remaining puppies, the breeder will be able to select the puppy best matched to your personality and home-life, obviously based on whether you want a male or a female, and color preferences.

The breeder will know the characters of their puppies better than anyone, so, unless you feel strongly about it, you would be advised to respect their judgment.

If the breeder is happy for you to pick your puppy, then one will usually steal your heart. To identify the puppy as yours, breeders often mark

The male (left) is a somewhat bigger, stockier dog than the female (right).

them temporarily – for example, by painting one of their claws a particular color, each owner having their own color code.

MALE OR FEMALE?

Which sex you would prefer is a matter of personal choice. Some people prefer females, others prefer males. Do not get a female with the intention that you can breed her – breeding is a science and should be left to the experts.

You should take into account that a female will come into heat around the age of six to nine months, and thereafter every six months (although every female is different). During this time, she will be irresistible to every dog within a considerable distance, who will all do everything in their power to get to her. She will also be desperate to meet up with her new admirers, and will need careful supervision to ensure she cannot escape. When she is in heat, she should not be walked in public places, where other dogs can gain access to her – garden exercise will have to suffice.

The males should look masculine, and the females should appear feminine. The males are a little bigger, stockier, and slightly more muscular than the females. There is not a significant size difference though.

If you do not intend to show your dog, you can consider neutering (altering). There are numerous health benefits of neutering, such as preventing pyometra (a life-threatening uterine infection) in the female and prostate disorders in the male. Your veterinarian will be happy to discuss neutering with you, and explain what is involved, when it should be done, and to help you to assess the risks and benefits.

COLOR

The U.K. Breed Standard lists four acceptable colors: silver, apricot, fawn, and black; the U.S. Standard lists three: silver, apricot-fawn, and black.

Silver is incredibly rare, and you are unlikely to find anyone that would let you have a genuine silver-coated dog (they are so unusual that the breeder would want to keep such a specimen for themselves!). In the U.K., apricot is a warmer version of the fawn. In the U.S., apricot-fawn counts as one color.

So, basically, you have two choices: fawn or black. A black coat should be black – not nearly black, brown, or with white. When you pick a puppy, you will not be able to guarantee that the fawn coat will remain fawn, or that the promising apricot one will ever develop, because the coat changes as the puppy matures. When they are born, all fawn Pugs appear to be very dark, nearly black. As they grow, the coat color becomes lighter, and you can usually tell the eventual color by about 12–14 weeks. A good indication is to look at the legs and feet – often the coat develops into these shades. If you don't base your choice of puppy on color alone, you won't be disappointed.

SHOW POTENTIAL

If you intend to show your Pug puppy, you should take the advice of your breeder, who will be able to spot a puppy with potential.

• The puppy should look like a miniature adult.

A puppy should look like a miniature version of the adult Pug.

- He should have a good-shaped head, large eyes, and small, button or rose ears.
- He should have a neat nose, but it should not be too narrow.
- The "twist" (tail) gets tighter as the puppy gets older, but it should already be curling by six weeks.
- The body should look sturdy and square.
- The front legs should look straight, and the hindlegs should be strong.
- The puppy should have good black pigment (nose, nails, eye line, and ears).

DOUBLE TROUBLE

Choosing a Pug is always a difficult decision – all the puppies look so cute! Resist any temptation to take two puppies. Training one Pug is hard enough – two Pugs are nearly impossible! Although they may look like adorable little angels, they can become naughty little demons when they want to be, and you really will have your work cut out. You might think that two Pugs mean double the pleasure, but really it will be double the trouble!

If you want two Pugs, wait until the first one is a couple of years old before getting another. This will give you time to properly train and socialize him before starting the process all over again.

WAITING GAME

After reserving your puppy, you will have to wait several weeks until he is old enough to be released by the breeder. The wait will seem a long one, and you will soon be counting the days until you can bring your little puppy home.

However, there's plenty that you can be doing to keep you occupied and to ensure that you will be fully prepared when your Pug puppy comes home.

SHOP 'TIL YOU DROP

Pug puppies may be small, but they still need an awful lot of stuff!

- Bed – should be warm, draft-free, comfortable, and easy to clean. For young puppies who are still being house-trained, a cardboard box with one side cut down makes a cozy retreat if lined with old blankets.
- Food and water bowls – there are lots of types on the market. Plastic is cheap and durable, but it scratches over time and will need to be replaced; stainless steel is durable; ceramic looks attractive but can smash.
- Collar and leash – choose a soft, comfortable collar that can be extended as your puppy grows. The leash should be light, so your puppy hardly notices he is on it (see page 53).
- Toys – there are many varieties, but buy only those that are durable and safe. Toys with removable parts should be avoided, as they can be swallowed.
- Crate – essential for all puppy owners (see page 31).
- Food – find out from the breeder what food the puppy is used to, and buy some. A change in diet can lead to tummy upsets (see page 55).
- Stair-gate – important for confining your puppy to a safe room in the house, and

barring access to the stairs (page 70).

- A soft brush and/or grooming glove (page 58).
- Toothbrush and dog toothpaste (page 62).
- Guillotine-type nail-clippers (page 62).

PUPPY-PROOFING

Before you bring home the puppy, you must make sure that your home and garden are completely safe for him. Crawl around your rooms one at a time to get a puppy's perspective. Are there any electrical cables he can chew? Can any knickknacks be knocked over? Are all house plants out of the way (some can be toxic to dogs)?

Check the garden for possible escape routes!

If you have children or an untidy spouse, warn them that anything that is left on the floor or within the puppy's reach is fair game. Usually, it takes at least one misdemeanor before this message is understood. Once an expensive pair of sneakers has been chewed or piddled on, it's amazing how quickly everyone suddenly remembers to be more careful about what is left out around the home.

Next, take a look at the yard. Again, crawl around to see if there are any holes in your fence or gate through which a puppy could escape. If you have a pond or a swimming pool, it should be covered, or fenced, so the puppy cannot investigate and get into trouble.

If you are an avid gardener, who would be distraught at the idea of a puppy chewing your prize veggie, or trampling over your beloved begonias, make sure your Pug cannot gain access to these areas.

Also make sure that your garden flowers are safe for dogs. As with house plants, some garden plants (such as ivy) can be toxic if chewed. If in doubt, ask the advice of your local garden center.

FINDING A VETERINARIAN

All veterinarians are skilled professionals who have undergone many years' training and education. Although they may be equally qualified, there are many other factors that may dictate your choice.

Personal chemistry

With some people, you hit it off right away.

With others, you can take an instinctive dislike to them. Your puppy's veterinarian must be someone who you can trust and get along with.

It is a very lucky pet owner that goes through 14 years without having at least a couple of anxious times with their pet's health. During these stressful situations, it is important to have complete confidence in the veterinarian. If you anticipate personality clashes, find someone else. Ideally, you will find a veterinarian that has experience in dealing with Pugs, or at least with Toy breeds.

When you visit different veterinary clinics, have a chat with some of the nursing and reception staff – you will be dealing with them too, and the nursing staff will be caring for your precious Pug. You should also find out about emergency cover, and the facilities available at the clinic.

Location

In emergencies, when every second counts, it is important that you can get to the veterinary clinic quickly and easily. Does it have its own parking area nearby?

Services

What, in addition to good health care, can the clinic offer you? If you would like to have the option of using complementary therapies, is there someone suitably qualified? Does the clinic have any special equipment? If you have an equal choice between a veterinarian that has his own testing equipment and one that has to send the samples away, choose the former – it produces faster results, saving you hours of anxiety while waiting.

Hours

What are the clinic's hours? Are they convenient for you? What will happen if you need a veterinarian outside these hours? In the U.K., it is a legal obligation that the clinic has a veterinarian on call 24 hours a day; in the U.S., clinics often form affiliations with other clinics in the area and do a rotation system between them. Ask if your clinic does the same.

JOURNEY HOME

Try to arrange to acquire the puppy from the breeder in the morning. This will give you plenty of time to travel home and get the puppy settled in before he is put to bed in the evening.

You will need someone to look after your puppy on the journey home.

Also arrange for someone to travel with you – ideally, someone who can drive so that you can hold and reassure the puppy on the return journey. Hold the puppy securely on your lap, and comfort him. You will also be free to clean up any accidents or car sickness that may occur. Place a thick, soft towel on your lap for the puppy to sit on (it will also help to protect you from any misdemeanors!).

If the weather is warm, ensure that the car interior is well ventilated, and make sure that the puppy has access to fresh water. If the journey is a long one, and you need to make a stop, ensure that your puppy does not come into contact with any other dogs or places where they may have been present. This even includes letting him walk on the ground – instead, carry him.

If your breeder has kept the puppy until 12 or 14 weeks of age, to ensure that he has been fully vaccinated before leaving (and that the vaccinations have been given time to become effective), then such precautions will not be necessary. Check this out with the breeder before leaving.

RESCUED DOGS

A number of Pugs end up in breed rescue and general rescue organizations every year. Usually, they are there through no fault of their own. As Sylvia Smith, Pug breed rescue coordinator in the U.K., explains, "Pugs are stoic little dogs, with lots of fun and energy. They are often portrayed in the media as old ladies' lapdogs, but this is not the case." According to Sylvia,

Sadly, far too many Pugs end up in rescue shelters.

Pugs often end up in rescue because elderly owners can no longer care for them properly, because their owners end up in residential centers where they are often unable to keep pets, or because the owner dies.

A small number are put up for rehoming because they become dirty in the house, through owners not taking them outside enough, or because the dogs are left for prolonged periods while owners are away at work.

Although Pugs are devoted little dogs who bond closely with their owners, they are surprisingly easy to rehome, taking to their new homes without a backward glance.

Within 48 hours, most Pugs will have settled down, and, within three weeks, they usually have won over every member of the family. As long as you love a Pug and feed him, he will give you his heart.

If you are interested in adopting a rescued Pug, you should contact your national breed club, which will provide you with the details of the breed rescue scheme.

As with buying a puppy, you should be able to provide the puppy with a stable, secure home, where the dog will never be left for more than four hours at a time.

After you apply, you will be assessed and home-checked, and, if considered suitable, put on a list of potential owners so that your details can be matched to a suitable dog.

When you bring your rescued Pug home, you shouldn't overwhelm him. Just let him have the run of the ground floor, and let him sniff around and investigate. Supervise him to make sure he doesn't do anything he shouldn't, but don't crowd him. Call him to you every now and again, and give him a gentle pet if he comes to you, but don't fuss over him. Give him a couple of days before you invite people to meet him.

If your Pug won't eat for the first 24 hours, don't panic. Dogs often lose their appetites if they are stressed. Within a day, when he's settled in and calmed down, his love of food will soon return. If his anorexia continues, however, you should seek veterinary advice.

PUG BOATS

Vivienne Gratton from Chesterfield, Derbyshire, in the U.K. is the lucky owner of Misty, a rescued dog. Misty was not in very good condition when she was rescued – she had trouble with her teeth and eyes, but is now in tip-top condition (although a little toothless).

Vivienne's other Pug, Monty, has accepted the newcomer with open paws, and adores his new housemate.

"At first, Monty made a bit of a nuisance of himself," explains Vivienne. "He seemed to think that Misty was there for his own personal pleasure! However, we soon put a stop to that, and now they eat from the same bowl, sleep in the same basket, and are utterly inseparable. Monty even pines for Misty if she is not around.

"We have our own boat, and have had little life-jackets made for the two dogs so they can come with us in safety. They lounge around on deck quite happily, and seem to enjoy themselves – they adore my husband and myself, and would much prefer to accompany us on the boat rather than be left at home. They follow us around everywhere and would shadow us to the ends of the earth if they had to."

Misty and Monty enjoying life on board.

PUG MAGIC

Pugs are captivating creatures, capable of casting a spell on their owners to win their hearts – and this is exactly what happened to Rosemary Cooper from Henley-on-Thames, Oxfordshire.

"My husband, Paul, has had Pugs for many years. Merlin was the first Pug we had together. We bought him as a puppy, and he was a wonderful dog," says Rosemary.

"One day, I read an article about rescued Pugs, and I rang up to find out more. After filling in the relevant forms and being assessed, several months later I received a call. Did we want a one-eyed, six-year-old Pug, who was fear-aggressive? No one else wanted him. Of course, we said 'yes' straight away."

BAD START

"I collected Theo and he sat contentedly on the front seat as we drove home. As I put my hand out to change gear, however, he leapt forward and fastened his teeth on my wrist! Not the best of starts!

"When he arrived home, he was starving, and I gave him lots to eat – which he promptly vomited in the middle of the dining-room carpet.

Theo: The one-eyed Pug that nobody wanted.

"Nearly six years on, now approaching 12 years of age, Theo is still as bloody-minded. But that's one of the things I love about Theo – he will never compromise. For example, he doesn't like being picked up. If you try it, he'll bite you. That's that! But his attitude to life is quite understandable when you consider everything he's been through.

"One of his former owners (and he had many in the first six years of his life) was an elderly lady who was quite frightened of him. She would throw a blanket over him before picking him up. It's no surprise that he doesn't like being picked up really, is it? Despite his faults, Theo is wonderfully rewarding and terribly affectionate; he looks at us with his one good eye, expressing total devotion – and at the same time worrying that his paradise may not last.

"Theo decided he was the top dog from the start, and tried to assert his authority over Merlin. However, Merlin remained quite aloof – he never thought of himself as anything other than a Pug and a Cooper, so didn't acknowledge this canine behavior."

STRONG BOND

"Our second rescued Pug is Edward. He was used as a stud dog, and was kept in a cage for the best part of three years. Theo attacked Edward straight away. The only possible answer was to have Theo neutered, which calmed him down. He still bullies Edward from time to time just to show who's boss.

"Edward looked slightly confused on the first night after arriving home, so I lay down on the floor with him, and we had a cuddle. When it was time to go into his crate for the night, I took off the sweater I had been wearing, put it inside his crate, and he slept on it all night through – we didn't hear a peep out of him. The bonding from that night has remained strong ever since – he's convinced I'm his mother!

Edward soon found his feet in his new home.

"Edward was never trained before he came to us – outside in a cage all day, there was no need. House-training will always be a problem for him. He's done his best to ruin our home, having peed on every scrap of carpet there is!

"Edward is a very greedy dog, as many Pugs are. One year, the table was laid for Christmas dinner, and he sat on a chair several yards away, looking. You could see him thinking, 'I might be able to manage this,' and, with a great leap, he did, landing right in the middle of all of it!

"Both dogs quickly worked out that when the fridge or dishwasher is open, there's a chance of food – they both do a very good 'first rinse' job in the dishwasher.

"Edward is unreservedly affectionate, and will always rush up to you and bring you a shoe or some other token when you come into the house. As a result, it's usually very difficult to find an intact pair when you want them!

"Edward has a contented view of the world – he will cuddle up on my lap and think, 'Now I know I'm in heaven!', whereas Theo is a bit more wary – he'll think, 'Now I know I'm in heaven! But will it last'?

"Although it hasn't been easy, I would certainly have another rescued Pug. They are plucky and so very rewarding. I was brought up on a farm in New Zealand, where we had perfectly-trained working sheepdogs. I can imagine my father (who died many years ago) looking down at me now, saying, 'That's not my daughter! Not with those ridiculous little dogs!'"

Theo and Edward have found love and contentment, the second time around.

CHAPTER THREE

ARRIVING HOME

After weeks of waiting, you finally have your new Pug puppy home with you. This is a big step for the puppy, who has only ever known one family before and will never yet have been separated from his siblings. It is important not to overwhelm him in the first few days – simply take things slowly, and plan your family introductions (human and animal) carefully – remember, first impressions count!

HOME AT LAST

After the journey, the puppy will probably need to relieve himself – especially with all the excitement of the day. Plus, having been confined in the car, he will need to stretch his legs. As soon as you arrive home, let him into your garden to have a good sniff and to exercise.

Wait until he relieves himself – as soon as he does so, give him plenty of praise and a treat (see page 46).

If you have a cat or another dog at home, keep them out of the way for the first couple of hours after bringing the pup home – faced with a new owner and a new home, the puppy will need a little time to settle down before the excitement of meeting his four-legged housemates.

Your puppy will probably need a meal soon after arriving home. Check the diet sheet that the breeder has supplied you with, and follow it to the letter. Afterward, take him outside to relieve himself once more, and then put him in his crate to have a nap.

CRATE-TRAINING

Crates are invaluable. They can be used for a number of purposes:

- To keep the pup safely out of harm's way at night when he cannot be supervised.
- If you need to leave him for short periods (to go shopping, for example).
- If you invite friends to the house who do not appreciate dogs.

Reassure your puppy when you put him in the crate.

Most puppies will soon learn to settle – particularly if you provide a toy to play with.

- To keep the puppy safe from other household pets and vice versa when you are not able to watch over them.

The crate should be large enough to accommodate a fully-grown adult (20 inches long, 14 inches wide, and 16 inches high is ideal – 50 cm x 35 cm x 40 cm). Put it in a quiet room in the house, where your pup won't be disturbed when he is resting – puppies, like babies, need plenty of rest.

Line the crate bottom with newspaper in case of accidents, and put a blanket over the top, so he has a warm, comfortable bed. Leave one end of the newspaper uncovered. Although your puppy should be toileted before being placed inside, and the crate should never be used for long periods, your puppy may be caught short

during the night. Puppies are preprogrammed not to relieve themselves near their beds, so leave him a small area of newspaper that he can use without compromising himself.

It is a good idea to have a familiar scent in his crate – some people take a soft towel or blanket to the breeder when they pick a puppy, and collect it when they take the puppy home. The puppy will associate the smell of his former home and family with being safe and secure, and it may help him to settle faster.

Put a safe chew-toy in the crate, put the puppy inside, and talk softly to him while petting him slowly. It won't be long before he drifts off to sleep.

Never use the crate for long periods. It should only be used for the odd hour when you cannot keep an eye on your puppy (or at night). It should not be used as a dogsitter, to keep your puppy from destroying your house while you go to work all day. A Pug needs company, and a puppy needs lots of interaction with people to help him grow into a happy, well-mannered dog.

NAME GAME

Some puppies' names come easily – they seem to have their names written on their faces and you know it as soon as you lay eyes on them. Others are more difficult to name.

You may have decided on a name before bringing the puppy home. If so, let the breeder know, so he or she can familiarize the puppy with it as early as possible.

It is important that the puppy learns to associate his name with good things. Say his name over and over, while you are cuddling him, just before you feed him and while he is eating, while you are playing with him, etc.

Never say his name when he is in the veterinary clinic, or at any other time when he may be stressed or unhappy. Never shout his name if you are cross with him – it is very important that, in the early months, his name signifies only good things.

MEETING THE FAMILY
Canine companions

Once your Pug awakes refreshed from his nap, take him outside to the garden for him to relieve himself once again. It is very important that he is given regular opportunities, in order to avoid accidents (see page 46).

If you have another dog, now would be a good time to let him meet the new arrival. A yard is a more neutral territory than a house – there is more room for them to check each other out, and avoid close contact if they don't want it, and your dog is likely to be less possessive about the yard. The ideal scenario would be for the two dogs to meet in a park (not one where your older dog is regularly walked). That way, no territorial issues will be at stake, and the dogs can make friends with each other before coming home together.

Little and large: The Pug is a sociable dog and will be happy to make friends – even if he is dwarfed by his canine companion.

Of course, this can only be done if your puppy is protected by his vaccinations (around 14 weeks of age). If this is not the case, the yard will have to suffice.

It is preferable to have both dogs off-leash when they meet. Leashes often embolden dogs, giving them the impression that they have to defend their owner or their space; and a tight leash can transmit tension to the dog. Off-leash, your older dog will be free to sniff out the newcomer and to walk away, as he sees fit.

Presumably, your older dog has an impeccable temperament with other dogs (if he doesn't, why would you take on a puppy?). Tempting though it is to interfere, it is best to let the two dogs get on with it. Dogs communicate with each other with great ease, and they will soon work out who's boss (usually the older dog). Your puppy will learn how to appease the top dog (for example, by averting his eyes when he growls, or rolling on to his back to show his submission). You'll have fun watching your two dogs' friendship develop – while learning a lot about canine behavior too.

With time, your older dog will realize that he has nothing to fear from the puppy, and they will soon become friends.

Remember: only intervene if the puppy is in serious danger (which is unlikely to happen if your older dog is well socialized). If the older dog growls, the puppy should take notice of him. If you butt in, you will upset the hierarchy that the dogs will be establishing, and both dogs will be confused. Dogs like order. The underdog is quite happy being inferior to the top dog, as long as he knows his place and what is expected of him.

Once the order has been established (and it isn't always the older dog that becomes boss – occasionally a puppy becomes top dog), you should reinforce what the dogs have agreed. Feed the top dog first, let him go through doors ahead of the other dog, etc. These actions may seem petty to us, but they are important indicators of status to dogs.

GREEN-EYED MONSTER

If you are introducing a new puppy or dog to the household, do not overlook your other pets. It's easy to make a big fuss of the newcomer to make him feel at home, but lots of attention should be given to the other animals in the house. If they feel neglected, they will resent the new dog – and you!

Inside the home, while still introducing your dogs and settling the newcomer in, confine the puppy, not the dog with seniority – otherwise resentment will result.

Feline friends

With a Pug's large, fairly prominent eyes, cats can pose a danger. A well-aimed swipe, and the eye could be permanently damaged. However, that doesn't mean that cat and Pug ownership is barred to you. Pugs are not cat-chasers at heart, so you won't be battling with the dog's basic instincts to make the relationship work. Plus, Pugs are pretty canny creatures, and soon realize what they can get away with. If the cat is hostile, they'll learn to leave well enough alone. If the cat is friendly, they'll be happy to share their

Supervise your Pug and your cat to begin with.

bed with their new companion. With careful handling, the two can become best buddies – it just takes some time, common sense, and the following tips:

- Introduce the Pug in a crate. Let the cat into the room to take a sniff. She will be able to investigate, while feeling secure that the puppy is not a threat – and, of course, the puppy will be safe from her claws.
- Reassure the cat, and, every few minutes, call her to you. To tempt her to you, show her some of her favorite treats (such as fresh chicken or a little pâté). She will begin to associate the puppy with tasty treats and will soon realize the puppy isn't a threat.
- After each of these crate introductions, keep the two pets separate, and reward each of them.
- After half a dozen of these meetings, the puppy and the cat will stop being novelties to each other, and won't take very much notice of the other.
- When it reaches this stage, take the puppy out of his crate, put him on your lap, and allow the cat to come into the room.

- Cats are very inquisitive, and she will probably come over to check him out now he isn't behind bars. Restrain the pup, and stroke him around the head (this way, you will be able to screen his eyes with your hand if puss attempts a clout).
- Talk calmly to both the puss and the pug.
- Periodically, give them treats to make the experience a rewarding one.
- Again, try a few of these introductions, so they become relaxed in each other's company.
- Next, cuddle with the cat on your lap. Ask a family member to let the puppy into the room. The cat should feel safe enough on your lap to watch the Pug playing in the room. If she doesn't feel happy, she will probably jump on the back of the sofa.
- This will be the first opportunity she will have had to see his movements. It won't take her long to figure him out and realize that he can't attack her.
- Cats usually growl and hiss before attacking. If it gets to this, whisk the pup out of the way. Once a pup has been hissed at, he'll be reluctant to bother the cat again.
- By diverting the cat's or the puppy's attentions, however – by calling them to you and giving them treats – conflict should be avoided.
- Never leave the two pets unsupervised. If you need to go out, put the puppy safely in his crate so he can't come to any harm – see page 31.
- Never rush any of the stages. If your cat feels threatened, she may lash out.

PERFECT PUG PARTNERS

If there is anyone that disproves the myth that Pugs and cats cannot live together in harmony, it is Lynne Whittaker from Sidcup, Kent, in the U.K. With many years' experience of living in a houseful of Pugs, Pekingese, and pusses, Lynne has cracked the secret of canine/feline success.

"I have had Pugs, Pekes, and cats for more than 40 years," explains Lynne. "Although my dogs have had eye injuries through their own stupidity (rushing about in the garden and not looking where they were going), or from the other dogs, none has ever had a cat-related injury. I've asked friends who own Pugs and cats, and they haven't experienced any trouble either."

Petal the cat has learned that Pugs are not such a bad thing….

SMART CATS

"I currently have 14 dogs, and they behave like a pack. If a cat runs, one will chase after it, and they all start following. My seven cats have learned to walk slowly when the dogs are about, or just avoid the ground altogether, and move around the house by leaping from one bit of furniture to another. The cats are smart and see that a group of mischievous, naughty Pugs and Pekes is something that is best avoided.

"When I had a smaller number of dogs, the situation was different. The dogs did not act like a pack, and interacted with the cats a lot more.

One of my cats, Petal, give birth to kittens with a Pug in the room – she wasn't bothered at all.

"The dogs and cats used to share their beds with each other, and there is a genuine fondness between them. My cat, Loot, went missing for a year. When she was finally returned to us, she was overjoyed to see my Pug, James. She nuzzled all around him – rubbing herself up against him, and purring madly. They were both really happy to see each other again – they were like long-lost friends."

AT HOME WITH MR. MAGOO

Pugs are good-natured, tolerant dogs who will live in harmony with most creatures, provided they are socialized with them from a young age.

Diane Timmis who lives in Stoke on Trent, Staffordshire, in the U.K., watches over a veritable menagerie of animals, who all cohabit peacefully. As well as 22 dogs (Pugs, Dachshunds, a Great Dane, and a German Shepherd), she has cats, rabbits, cockerels, hens, turkeys, and tortoises!

Mr. Magoo, the turkey, rules the roost in Diane's mixed menagerie of pets.

"All puppies are playful and want to chase other animals, but the important thing is to never let this 'game' start. I tell them 'No, leave it!' sternly and they stop," says Diane.

"They grow up to respect each other. In time, they develop friendships, which can become very deep-seated. The funniest relationship has developed between one of my Pugs and Mr. Magoo, the turkey. I think it's got to the stage where the Pug thinks she's a turkey!"

Child's play

With many Toy breeds, children are a no-no. Some breeds are so small and fragile that kids are just too big a safety risk. However, the Pug is an exception.

Pugs are playful, lively little souls and love being involved in family life. Being young at heart, they can make good companions for well-behaved children – provided some basic rules are set, and then followed, such as:

The Pug is a lively, playful dog who enjoys the company of children.

KIDS AT HEART

Breeder Sarah Hayward has a very successful show career with her Jansara Pugs (see page 107), but she manages to juggle this with raising two small children and teaching them to respect the breed.

"I was brought up with dogs," says Sarah, from Mosterton, Dorset in the U.K., "and I began showing at the age of 11, so I had Pugs long, long before I had children. Pugs are my hobby and my life, so it has always been the case that any children I had would have to put up with the dogs!

"Fortunately, my children, Katie (five years) and Jade (two years) love the dogs, and the dogs love them. I think Pugs are one of the better breeds to have as a family dog, as they are fun and good-tempered – they would never bite or snap.

"Pugs are such great characters. They are really good fun – like children at heart. I have six Pugs and the younger ones especially love playing with Katie and Jade. It's important that they have time-out from each other, though. I have a stair-gate across the kitchen door; the dogs have the kitchen, utility room, and the garden, and the kids have the rest of the house. That way, the dogs are not hassled by the children all day, every day – only for controlled, supervised periods.

"Both children are very fond of the dogs, but, being that little bit older, Katie is especially attached to them. She has a special relationship with Milly, who has bonded closely with her. Whenever Katie walks into a room, Milly will stand up and is immediately attentive – she seems to think that Katie is her special owner.

"Both children have been taught to respect the dogs, and they wouldn't dream of pulling their tails. Certainly, the Pugs love Katie and Jade. When they are in the garden, they are always surrounded by the dogs. Pugs just love being with people and make excellent companions."

Katie and Jade love playing with the family Pugs.

- Never disturb the puppy when he is resting. Puppies need lots of sleep; when he is in his crate or bed, he must be left alone.
- All contact with the dog must be gentle. Play must not become boisterous, nor should the puppy be expected to play for hours on end.
- Stroke rather than pat. Children should be taught how and where to pet the puppy (e.g. stroking the top of the head and back, rather than hefty pats on the face).
- Consider the puppy at all times – e.g. there should be no running around when he is in the room. Accidents can happen, but many are avoided through common sense and care.
- If toys are not being played with, they should be put away. Anything left within the puppy's reach is up for being chewed, plus some toys (for example, those with removable parts) can be dangerous to the pup.
- Never share your food with the dog. Pugs live for their stomachs; once they have been given food from your plate, they will live in eternal hope that you will relent again. Then, they will beg at every mealtime, patrol under the table for any dropped bits, and generally make a nuisance of themselves. If they are never fed from the table, they will never expect to be.
- Children and dogs should never be left unsupervised.
- All friends should be taught the puppy rules when they visit.

It is important that the children know the rules before the puppy comes home. When they first meet the puppy, they will be very excited, but try to keep them calm. Everyone should sit on the floor and wait for the puppy to come to them. Give the children some treats to give to the puppy periodically, so he learns to associate them with a pleasant experience.

If the puppy chews their clothes, or gives them a nibble, they should squeal in a high-pitched voice and turn away from the puppy. This teaches the puppy that chewing kids is no fun, and results in being ignored – something the Pug really hates.

It is important to share the puppy's care with the children. They should be involved in his training, feeding, and walking – all under supervision, of course. Including all members of the family in the puppy's life will prevent him from becoming a one-person dog, and will also teach your children about the responsibility of pet ownership.

If you do not have children of your own, enlist some from friends – kids do not usually need to be asked twice, and it is important that your puppy is socialized with children from an early age (see page 43).

FIRST NIGHT

Don't expect to get too much sleep for the first couple of nights after bringing your Pug home. After spending all his life with his mother and littermates in the familiar home of the breeder, sleeping alone for the first time in a strange home can be upsetting for him. He is likely to cry for his family – and a Pug's cries can be truly heart-wrenching.

- Make sure your Pug is comfortable before settling him in his crate. Feed him his night-time snack (if advised on the diet sheet), let him outside to relieve himself, cuddle together quietly to make him drowsy, and then lay him in his crate, nestled in some soft bedding.
- Leave a ticking clock in the room – some owners claim the sound reminds the puppy of his litter's heartbeats, and this may help to reassure him.

It is inevitable that your puppy will feel lost and bewildered to begin with.

- Fill a hot-water bottle with warm water, wrap it in a thick towel, and place it in the puppy's bedding. After snuggling up with his mother and littermates, he should find the gentle warmth comforting.
- Once you put the puppy in his crate, shut the door, leave the room, and don't return to him until the morning. This may sound harsh, but it is best to get the puppy used to sleeping on his own from the start.
- Although it is tempting to comfort him when he cries, he may learn that yelping results in being cuddled – hardly an incentive to settle! If your puppy gets used to the nighttime routine from the very start, it will only be a matter of days before he is quiet through the night.
- If you (or your neighbors!) cannot cope with a howling puppy through the night, then talk to the puppy and try to settle him back to sleep. Do not overexcite him by playing with him or cuddling him. However, the best option is to try to ignore him – after a couple of nights he should be quiet throughout the night.
- However tired you are, try to avoid taking the puppy to bed with you. You will start a habit you will have to live with, as your Pug will spend every night scrabbling at your bedroom door to enjoy it again and again. Of course, if you want to spend the next 14 years or so with your Pug on (or in!) the bed, that's fine – just be aware that many are expert snorers!
- Get him up first thing in the morning so you

can take him outside for toilet training. A puppy cannot hold on for any length of time, and it is cruel to expect him to cross his legs or to soil his crate just so that you can have an extra half-hour in bed.

VETERINARY VISIT

Arrange for your puppy to have a complete veterinary exam the day after you bring him home. The veterinarian will advise you about microchipping (a permanent form of identification where a small chip giving your contact details is inserted under the skin), vaccinations, worming, neutering, and general care. Remember to take along details of treatments the puppy has received so far from the breeder.

It is important that your puppy sees the veterinarian as a great person to meet, as this is the start of a lifelong relationship. Take along some extra-special treats that the veterinarian can give the puppy. You may find the veterinarian has got there first, and already has some treats to offer. Take your time talking to the veterinarian so he has the opportunity to stroke your puppy and get to know him. If they bond now, it will make life much less stressful in the future.

The veterinarian will give your Pug a thorough checkup to ensure that he is in good health.

CHAPTER FOUR

EARLY LESSONS

I n the same way that the child is father to the man, so the puppy is father to the dog. If you work hard, socializing and training your Pug when you first bring him home, you will reap the rewards when your dog blossoms into a well-mannered, trustworthy, loving adult companion. Fail to invest in your pup's future, and you will regret it for the rest of his life.

Many people think that small dogs don't need to be trained – reasoning that they can't do the damage that unruly larger dogs can. Not true! A yappy, nippy dog is not a joy to live with, and can inflict damage – why put up with it when you can have a well-behaved companion?

Others say that Toy breeds can't be trained. More untruths! This is a major injustice to all Toy dogs, and to Pugs in particular. Pugs are intelligent dogs – more clever than many give them credit for. There is ample evidence of this in chapter seven. As you will no doubt soon find out, you should never underestimate a Pug!

SOCIALIZATION

Exposing your puppy to as many experiences as possible is the most important thing you can do for your Pug. Puppies are pretty fearless souls that exude confidence – if they encounter something new, they will be inquisitive rather than afraid. This positive attitude gradually declines as the puppy matures, however, so it is important to introduce him to many everyday sights and sounds early, so that he considers them part of normal life.

If your breeder keeps the puppy until after the vaccinations become effective, it is important that he or she starts the socialization program. If you have the puppy before his vaccinations, early (and continuing) socialization is your responsibility.

- After the puppy has settled in for a couple of days, invite different people around to meet him – new people every day.
- He should get used to being handled by

Your puppy needs to get used to being handled by different people.

people of different ages, sexes, and ethnic backgrounds. If people cuddle him and give a treat when they first meet him, he will always think positively of strangers in the future.

- Every day, introduce your puppy to at least half a dozen new things – personal stereos, mobile phones, umbrellas, people wearing hats and motorcycle helmets, people playing musical instruments or rollerblading – use your imagination. All this will prepare the puppy for when he is finally allowed to go out into the larger world.

- With each experience, act calmly so the puppy doesn't detect any negative vibes from you. If you are confident, he will realize there is nothing to fear.

- Does your veterinary clinic organize puppy parties? These provide the opportunity for clients' dogs to meet each other and learn vital social skills, as well as having the chance to get to a new environment.

- If you bought a home-reared puppy from the breeder, as advised, he should be used to vacuum cleaners, the sound of aerosols, washing machines, hairdryers, etc. Make sure he continues to encounter all these items so that he doesn't develop any sudden fears of them through underexposure.

CAR TRAVEL

It is also important to get your puppy used to car travel – it should prevent him from becoming a nervous, sick passenger in the future. It is a good way of introducing him to the big, wide world before his vaccinations take effect. He will get used to the sound of traffic, car horns, emergency-service sirens, and so on.

- Secure your puppy in his crate, and place it in the back of the car. Car harnesses that clip into the rear seat belts are also available for dogs.

- Regularly take him out for short rides (gradually increasing the length of the journey as the puppy gets more relaxed).

- Talk to him throughout the journey to reassure him.

- Avoid car sickness by taking him out before meals; feed him when you return home, as a reward for the journey. This will help him to associate the car journey with something enjoyable – many dogs think all trips mean a visit to the veterinarian!

- It is perfectly normal for a puppy to be car-sick. With short, frequent trips he should overcome this. If the car sickness doesn't disappear, give the puppy a ginger cookie shortly before a journey – ginger is a natural remedy for this condition.

HOT DOGS

Never leave a dog unattended in a car – whatever the weather. Many dogs are stolen each year, and many more are killed through overheating. Even on an overcast day, the temperature inside a car can rise rapidly and kill a dog – especially a flat-faced Pug.

Most Pugs love the car, and love to be included on outings.

THE OUTSIDE WORLD

Once your puppy's vaccinations have taken effect, take him out to as many places as you can. With each encounter (human, canine, or other), keep his leash loose and remain calm and happy so your puppy picks up on your positive attitude.

- Go shopping together – sit in malls or on park benches and watch the world go by. If anyone shows interest in the puppy (many will!), let them pet him, and give them a treat to feed to him.
- Go on the train, bus, and subway (regulations permitting) together.
- Walk under ladders and over bridges.
- Take him to the beach (regulations permitting).
- Carry him when you go up an escalator.
- Walk him near an airport where he can get used to low-flying planes.
- Use your imagination – think of all the things your Pug may experience in his lifetime and try to cram in as many experiences as possible while he is still a puppy.

TRAINING

Join a training class as soon as it is safe for your puppy to do so. Choose a club that uses only kind, effective, reward-based methods – if choke chains are used, or the dogs are shouted at or smacked, walk away. Visit one of the classes before taking your dog along, to make sure they are well organized and that, initially, all the puppies are in approximately the same age group.

Okay, so it is unlikely that your Pug will become an Obedience Champion, but the classes will be fun for your dog and provide excellent socialization with other dogs of all breeds and types.

The classes will also be enjoyable for you – they will improve the bond you have with your dog, and will provide you with the opportunity of chatting with other puppy owners too.

If you remember to take your puppy outside at regular intervals, he will soon get the hang of house-training.

HOUSE-TRAINING

Puppies are generally very clean animals, and are preprogrammed to be house-trained. For wild dogs and wolves – all ancestors of your little Pug – house-training is a matter of survival. Feces and urine in the den could lead to ill health in the litter, and the scent could also bring predators. Tiny puppies are therefore cleaned by their mothers; as soon as they are able to move around, they instinctively crawl away from their sleeping area to relieve themselves.

However, Pugs are notoriously difficult to house-train, though this does not mean that it is an impossible task. It just takes patience and a regular routine.

When you take your pup home, your job is to show him that the entire house is his den and should not therefore be soiled. Instead, you will need to provide him with a suitable toileting area outside.

House-training isn't rocket science; if you follow some basic rules, you will have a clean puppy in no time at all.

It may sound obvious, but the key to success is to avoid accidents at all costs. Not only will they undermine your hard work, but, the more accidents occur, the more likely they are to happen again in the future. Avoiding accidents reinforces the correct behavior you want to encourage. If you stick to a routine, the puppy won't have any opportunity to be incontinent. Take your puppy outside to a designated toileting area at frequent intervals, including:

- First thing in the morning
- After meals
- Before and after naps
- Following periods of excitement (e.g. meeting new people, play)
- Every two hours (more if accidents persist)
- Last thing at night before settling him in the crate/bed
- Whenever you spot one of the warning signs (see page 47).

Stay outside with the puppy until he performs. Don't distract him by playing with him, just be around. As soon as he starts relieving himself, say a command, such as "Get busy." In time, he will associate the words with the action, and you will be able to get him to perform on command.

Once he has finished, give him lots of praise, a treat, and then play a game together in the yard. This will show the puppy that you are very pleased with him, and he will soon realize that relieving himself outside, on the chosen toileting spot, results in good things happening.

Never return directly indoors afterwards. Clever Pug puppies soon realize that relieving themselves results in being taken indoors, and so learn to keep their legs crossed for as long as possible!

After a few weeks, encourage your Pug to use different surfaces – gravel, concrete, grass, sand, and so on. Some become fussy about only relieving themselves on one type of surface – which can be a nightmare if you ever change your routine, or have a day out somewhere where that surface is not available!

Don't become too complacent too soon. Maintain a strict schedule even if your puppy has been clean for weeks. If you begin to skip toilet breaks, do not be surprised if your puppy lapses. The world is an exciting place for a fun-loving Pug puppy – he has far better things to do than to remember boring things like when to go to the toilet! Do your puppy's thinking for him until he is at least five or six months old – longer if he still needs it – and never leave the puppy unsupervised around the house (for safety's sake and to watch for any accidents).

Dealing with accidents

You will be exceptionally lucky if your Pug doesn't have at least a few accidents. Although they can be irritating, there's no need to get worked up about them. Just clean them up thoroughly and resolve to take your puppy out more frequently in the future.

Rubbing the dog's nose in his mess or shouting at him is not only cruel, it is also futile. The puppy will not be able to associate something he may have done 10 minutes ago with your actions now. Plus, any form of punishment will ruin your relationship with your people-loving Pug. Instead, your partnership should be built on trust and understanding.

Once accidents happen, you should be more vigilant about them not happening again. Your puppy is likely to return to the spot of his first misdemeanor, so use a warm-water solution of biological washing powder to the clean the area thoroughly. This will remove all scent of the accident – ordinary disinfectants just mask the smell, which can still be detected by a dog's sensitive nose.

Warning signs

Puppies are very predictable creatures. When they are about to go to the toilet, they will sniff the ground, focus on a particular spot, and circle around it, before lowering themselves on to it.

As soon as you notice one of these warning signs, clap your hands and call your puppy's name. This should stop him in his tracks. Then call him outside, using any trick in the book – rustling a bag of treats, squeaking one of his favorite toys, anything that will persuade him outside. Then let him perform outdoors and praise lavishly.

COLLARED!

Get your puppy used to wearing a collar from an early age. It must be soft, light, and

Your puppy needs to get used to wearing a collar.

comfortable to wear. Remember to extend the collar as your puppy grows. As a general rule, you should be able to fit two fingers under the collar when it is fastened. Fix a tag on to the collar, giving your contact details in the event of the dog getting lost. Most pet stores have an instant engraving service.

- Have a collar ready by your armchair to put on your puppy when he is enjoying cuddling on your lap.
- When he is relaxed and sleepy, gently put the collar on him (making sure you can easily fit two fingers underneath it), and pet him.
- He is unlikely to realize the collar is on him initially. When he does become aware of it, he may scratch at it or rub himself against things in an effort to remove it.
- If he is troubled by it, distract him. Call his name, ask him to "Come," and play a game together. If he's having fun, he'll forget the collar.
- After a few minutes, remove the collar, and put it back on him in an hour or so. With repeated exposure to it, and if wearing the

collar is accompanied by treats or games, he will soon stop trying to remove it.
- Never leave the puppy unsupervised when he is wearing a collar. It could get caught on something and strangle him.

CLICKER TRAINING

This is an exciting new method of training, originally developed to train dolphins. The clicker is a small plastic box, with a metal tongue, which, when pressed with the thumb, makes a "click" sound.

The click should be made the instant the dog does something desirable, and then a treat and praise can be given. The dog then associates the sound with a reward, and will start to work hard to earn it.

The clicker is readily available in pet shops, and more clubs are using this method of training. It's simple and effective – try it yourself. Practice some of the exercises in this chapter, using a click-treat instead of the usual treat-only reward.

SIT

This is a handy exercise to teach, which can be used in a number of situations. It is especially useful to get your dog to sit quietly as you are preparing his meal (rather than dancing at your feet and tripping you in the kitchen), and to keep him still while you are grooming him. It may seem an impossible task to get your active little Pug to sit still for even a second, but, with practice and patience, he will be sitting on command with ease.

- Hold out a treat or a toy to your Pug. When

Hold a treat above your puppy's head to lure him into the Sit.

Give lots of praise when he is in the correct position.

he shows an interest in what you have, his head will follow it.

- Keep the treat close to his nose, and move your hand up and back, so that he has to stretch his neck up and back a little to reach it. He can only do this successfully if he puts his bottom on the floor.

- As soon as he sits, say "Sit." Then give lots of praise, and give him the treat or toy he has worked so hard for.

- Practice little and often throughout the day. Pugs love their treats, and it won't take him long to work out what you want him to do. Within just half a dozen sessions, he should be sitting quicker. Eventually, he will sit when you say the command word.

- Once he has learned this exercise, keep it fresh in his mind by asking him to sit when you put his leash on, before you give him a meal, etc.

TREATS ARE FOOD

When training your Pug, take any reward treats from the dog's daily food allocation, so he doesn't pile on the pounds.

DOWN

This is taught along the same lines as the Sit command – by luring the dog into position with a treat. A food treat is preferable to a toy in this exercise, as it can easily be held in the hand and

Lower a treat, and your pup will follow it, going into the Down position.

only given to your dog when you want to release it. Choose something smelly, such as liver and garlic treats. Most dogs will jump through hoops for this, and it will keep him enthusiastic even when he can't see it.

- Ask your Pug to "Sit" (page 48).
- Show him the treat, and, as his head attempts to follow it, bring your hand down to the ground so that it is about six inches (14.5 cm) in front of him.
- Hold the treat in the palm of your hand, facing downward. This way, it will be hidden from the puppy, and he will have to get right down to get his nose low.
- He is likely to stand up and bend down to reach the treat, but will soon realize that he can't get the treat from you.
- Eventually, he will try another tactic – lying down to get a better angle.
- As soon as he lies down, say "Down" and release the treat.
- Next time, it won't take him so long to work it out.

COME

This is one of the most important exercises you can teach your dog, enabling you to bring him to your side whenever he is within earshot.

Start teaching this exercise in the first few days of bringing your puppy home. Pug puppies love following their owners around the house – they aren't companion dogs for nothing! – so exploit this instinct to teach him the Come (Recall) exercise.

- Enlist the help of a friend or family member to put your dog in the Sit position and to gently restrain him.
- Position yourself a couple of yards (meters) in front of the puppy, facing toward him.

It is important to build up an enthusiastic response to the "Come" command.

Remember to give lots of praise when your puppy comes in to you.

- Call his name, followed by "Come," lean forward, and open your arms to him.
- Your helper should release the puppy, so he can run straight to you.
- Give him lots of praise and a cuddle when he comes.
- Keep practicing this exercise, gradually increasing the distance between the two of you.
- Always call your puppy to you in a friendly, excited tone of voice. Show him a treat or a toy if he is reluctant to come – and make sure you give him a really good reward every time he successfully comes to you.
- When he comes reliably, add some variety to keep the command fresh – call him from one room to another, from indoors to outdoors,

etc. Always give lots of praise when he comes – if there isn't a happy, smiley face and a petting waiting for him, why should he bother to put himself out?

When your dog is able to be exercised in public places, do not expect his recall to be as good as it is in his own house or yard. You will be competing with lots of new sights and smells, so you must be more exciting than ever to get your dog's attention and to encourage him to come.

Put your Pug on an extendable leash, and only let him off if you are certain that, despite what is going on around him, he will reliably return to you. Don't rely on being able to outrun your dog – Pugs can run faster than you think when they put their minds to it, and can often outwit those in pursuit!

STAY

Getting any puppy to stay is difficult – when they are awake, they are generally moving! However, this exercise is even more difficult for a Pug, a breed that loves being close to his owners.

- Stand directly in front of your Pug, and ask him to go Down (see page 49).
- Bend forward slightly, and hold your hand out, with your palm facing the dog.
- Say "Stay" in an authoritative tone.
- Wait for a count of three, and then praise your dog and give him a treat.
- Practice little and often, and gradually increase

The Stay exercise should be built up in easy stages.

the level of difficulty. Start by taking a step away from the dog. Count to three, then step forward to him and praise/treat him (always walk to him – if you call him to you, it will encourage him to break his Stay).

- Over time, extend the length of the Stay, and the distance between you both.
- Don't make the mistake of trying to do too much too soon. For example, once you've mastered one step away for 10 seconds, try two steps away at five seconds. Then build up to two steps at 10 seconds.
- If your pup comes to you, remain calm. Simply put him back in position and start again. Whatever you do, don't get cross – it will make your dog anxious, and he will be more likely to break the Stay again.
- If your dog makes a mistake, go back a stage, and only increase the difficulty once he has mastered the previous one.
- Once Down-stays are easy, then practice Sit-stays.

STAND

Whether your dog is destined for the show ring or not, the Stand position is always useful. It will mean your dog can be examined all over by a veterinarian, and will make grooming easier too.

- Put your puppy on a table in front of you.
- Gently place his legs in the correct Stand position, with the legs four-square.
- Say "Stand," praise him, and give a treat.
- Practice little and often, and, as he gets used to what is expected of him, make him wait a little longer before giving him the treat.
- With time, the dog should get into position whenever you ask him to Stand, and will wait patiently without fidgeting.
- It goes without saying that you should never leave the puppy or dog unsupervised on the table – even for a split-second.

Reward your puppy with a treat as soon as he stands still.

LEASH-TRAINING

Leash-training isn't usually a problem with the Pug, as it is, for example, with a Siberian Husky, who is large, powerful, and bred to pull. The main problem is making sure the dog is close to you, but not in danger of being stepped on. With practice, you will soon get into your own style of leash-walking, naturally falling into the right position.

- When your puppy is finally used to his collar (above), attach a lightweight leash to it and follow him around as he investigates or plays in the yard.
- Keep the leash very loose, so no pressure is exerted.
- Puppies can panic if the leash goes tight, and tend to do kangaroo impressions, leaping about frantically to get free. If the leash is loose, they will not realize they are even on the leash.

After a few of these practice sessions, encourage the puppy to walk beside you.

- Hold a toy or a treat out for him, next to your left leg. Wiggle it to persuade the puppy to follow it.
- Take five or six slow steps forward, holding the toy out just in front of the puppy's nose.
- As he walks beside you, say "Heel," then stop, and give him the toy or treat as a reward.
- Practice little and often, and, as your Pug improves, gradually introduce changes of pace and direction.

- If your Pug pulls ahead, come to a sudden stop. Then call him back to your side, and start again. He will soon realize that pulling is counterproductive – instead of him getting somewhere more quickly (the reason why he is pulling), it actually takes longer.
- Whenever your puppy is walking next to you, say "Heel" so he associates the word with the action. With time, you will be able to get him to walk to heel simply by giving him the Heel command as needed.

At first, you should do all your training in the yard or indoors. Only when your Pug has mastered the exercise (and once he is protected by all his vaccinations), should you practice in a park or other public place where there are likely to be more distractions.

Praise your dog excitedly, and reserve extra-tasty treats for these times, in order to maintain your dog's focus on you.

You can use a treat to encourage your puppy to walk on the leash.

CHAPTER FIVE

CARING FOR YOUR PUG

Compared with some breeds, Pugs are relatively low-maintenance. However, they do require some regular, basic care to keep them happy, healthy, and handsome.

FEEDING

Your dog's breeder (or rescue shelter) should provide you with comprehensive feeding instructions, explaining what should be fed, how much, and when. These should be followed to the letter, as a change in diet can cause stomach upsets.

Initially, your puppy will be on at least four meals a day. This will provide him with a steady source of fuel throughout the day, and is easier for him to cope with than digesting one big meal a day.

Gradually, as he gets older, these can be reduced to three meals a day. Your dog will start to show less interest in one of his meals, or not manage to finish up all of his food, at which time you can increase the amounts fed in the other three sessions and cut one meal out completely. Give your Pug the same daily ration, but split it into three meals instead of four.

A further meal can be cut out some weeks later so that, by the time your puppy is six months old, he will be on two meals a day – breakfast and supper. As before, more food should be given at these times to compensate for the lost meal.

No two Pugs are the same, of course. Some Pugs remain on three meals all their lives; the majority have two meals; and some have just one. Generally, it is preferable to give two meals a day to small breeds such as the Pug. Plus, being so food-obsessed, it makes their day doubly enjoyable.

Older dogs have their own specific dietary needs – see page 63.

TYPES OF FOOD

There are many, many types of dog food on the

Many brands have various life-stage types for puppies, adolescents, adults, and older dogs, to cater for a dog's changing nutritional needs. Some even have specific Toy varieties. If you are overwhelmed by the number of types offered, take advice from your dog's breeder.

Some people prefer to feed a home-prepared fresh diet of meat and fresh vegetables. Consult your veterinarian if you are planning to do this, and he or she will be able to guide you on catering for your dog's complex nutritional needs. Without guidance, you could malnourish your Pug.

OBESITY

Pugs love their food, and will seek it out wherever it is. If you are eating a meal, you will usually find a Pug at your feet, waiting for any dropped bits or for you to give in to his hard stare and give him something from your plate. Do not be tempted to relent, however. Once the dog has received food this way, he will continue to beg for the rest of his life, hoping that you will relent again. Plus, of course, snacking between meals is a big no-no, one that will result in your dog piling on the pounds.

Pugs are muscular, bulky dogs, but they should not carry any excess body fat. Obesity puts undue pressure on your dog's joints and heart, which will affect his quality of life – and possibly the length of it. Do not kill your dog with kindness. There are other, healthier ways of showing your dog that you love him – such as playing a game with his favorite toy, or petting him on your lap.

Most Pugs love their food; the hardest task is ensuring that your dog does not become obese.

market – from canned food that is fed with biscuits, to dry, complete foods that contain everything a dog needs. Dogs generally prefer wet foods, but there are many advantages to dry: they help to remove plaque from the teeth and there is no fuss – you just weigh out the amount you need and put it in your dog's dish. It is clean to use, easy to store, and has a longer shelf-life once opened than wet food. If you feed a dry, complete diet, do choose one that has small, bite-sized pieces, which are easier for your Pug to manage.

Weight increase often occurs gradually and unnoticeably. Owners are usually the last people to realize that their Pug needs a diet. The only way to keep an accurate track of his weight is to put him on the scales once a month.

If your Pug is overweight, you should reduce the amount of food he is eating, and you may also consider changing the type of food to a diet/lite variety. If the weight just isn't shifting, ask your vet's advice. Many clinics also run weight-advice sessions and regular weigh-ins.

CHEWS AND TREATS

Pugs are great chewers – and often have expensive tastes. Antique furniture and first-edition books are Pug favorites, so make sure you provide a cheaper, safer alternative for your dog to gnaw on.

Your Pug will enjoy a chew or a knuckle-bone – particularly when he is teething.

Large chews are enjoyed by Pugs. They help to alleviate boredom during quiet times, and also help to control plaque build-up on the teeth. Nylon-type bones are popular, but avoid small, thin chews that can get lodged in the dog's throat.

CHANGING A DIET

You are advised to stick to the diet that was recommended by your dog's breeder or rescue center. If you need to make changes (for example, if you are having difficulty getting hold of the recommended brand), then this should be done very gradually to avoid your Pug developing a tummy upset.

Just put a spoonful of the new food into his meal, and a spoonful less of the former food. After a couple of days, put two spoonfuls of the new food in, and reduce the former food by a corresponding amount, until, over the course of a couple of weeks, a complete changeover has been made.

EXERCISE

A puppy's exercise should be strictly controlled. Strenuous activity (such as excessively long walks, or running up and down the stairs) can contribute to joint problems, so stick to gentle play. Until the age of five months, unrestricted access to the garden for free-running should be all that is necessary. Leash-walking (see page 53) can then be introduced gradually (initially on grass before moving on to harder surfaces).

Pugs do not require a great deal of exercise, but they do need more than you would think.

You should aim at giving an adult Pug two 20-minute walks a day, together with free access to a well-fenced, secure garden.

In warm weather, you should adjust the times of your walks so your dog is not exercising in the heat. Walk him a little earlier in the morning, and later in the evening.

Most Pugs also dislike inclement weather, and may refuse to go outside at all in such conditions.

For winter, consider investing in a warm, waterproof coat for your dog (there are lots of designs to choose from), which may persuade him to leave the comfort of his home for a quick stroll. Windy weather is best avoided – it plays havoc with a Pug's sensitive eyes.

Pugs enjoy their exercise – but take care that your dog does not become overheated in warm weather.

If it is very wet, cold, or gusty, take your Pug to a sheltered area to do his business (and stay with him all the time) and then take him back indoors if he doesn't want to remain outside. Instead, play some indoor games together so he doesn't become a couch potato.

Always keep a close eye on your Pug during walks to ensure he is breathing easily and is not getting overheated. Pugs will rarely give up on a walk – and will struggle to keep up with their beloved owners.

GROOMING

Being companion dogs, Pugs enjoy being gently groomed – it's just another form of stroking to them, and they always revel in being given attention.

Brushing the coat with a soft bristle brush or hound glove, for just a few minutes each day, stimulates the bloodflow to the skin, and keeps the coat in top condition. It also gives you an opportunity to check the dog's body for any lumps, cuts, grass seeds, parasites, and so on.

Fawn dogs generally have a double coat, but black dogs generally have a single coat, and the hair is slightly finer in texture. A casting coat can be improved by gently raking it out every day (Take care to ensure that the rake doesn't scratch the skin.)

Regular brushing will control the amount of shed hair that ends up in your home and on your clothes. Traditionally, Pugs shed in the spring and autumn (fall), but it is dependent on the temperature (a warm autumn or cold spring can delay the coat change). A female may also shed around the time of going into heat.

Tip: In good weather, brush your dog outdoors to keep your carpet and furnishings free of excess hair.

EARLY START

Your Pug should get used to a daily grooming routine from a young age.

- Place a towel or a rubber mat on a table or other waist-high surface (this will save you from having to stoop over your dog while you are grooming or checking him), and place him on it. Reassure your pup, so he does not try to leap off the table.
- Gently groom him all over, all the time telling him he is a very good dog.

- Give him a treat, and lots of praise.
- Next, get him used to being examined all over – check his eyes, nose, and inside his ears.
- Now for the tricky bit – feet! Pugs are renowned for their ticklish toes, so it is important to get him accustomed to this part of the routine very early on. After touching the feet for just a few seconds, give an extra-special treat and lots of attention. Over several sessions, touch the feet for longer periods.
- Finally, brush his teeth gently (see page 62).
- At the end of every session, give him lots of praise, a treat, and play a fun game together as a reward.
- It will be helpful to teach your puppy the "Stand" and "Down" commands, so you can put him into the most convenient position for the work you are doing (see pages 49 and 52).

Start by giving a few strokes with the brush, giving your puppy lots of praise for standing still.

Pugs can be sensitive about having their feet touched, so practice from an early age.

BATHING

Although Pugs hate getting wet on walks, most love to be bathed – after all, being bathed in warm water in a warm room is definitely better than getting cold and muddy outside! Plus, of course, they also adore being the center of attention.

Some people bathe their Pugs in a sink. This is fine if your shower attachment will reach (there probably won't be room for it to fit in the sink with your dog). An alternative is to raise your dog up in the bath – a small plastic table will allow you to reach your dog easily, use the bath shower attachment, and avoid backache!

Bathe your Pug as necessary. Some require just a couple of baths a year, while others are mucky little souls that need a dip in the tub once a month. If a mild dog shampoo is used, it shouldn't ruin the coat, as can happen in some breeds. A harsh shampoo will strip the natural oils from the coat, so use a gentle variety.

- Making sure that your dog's eyes are shielded, wet the coat thoroughly with warm (not hot) water.
- Apply the shampoo as directed on the label (often, it needs to be mixed with a little water before it is applied to the coat).
- Massage into a rich lather, working into the coat, down to the skin, and all over the dog's body.
- Thoroughly rinse away all the suds (again, being careful that none get into the eyes).
- Wrap your dog in a towel, remove him from the bath, and rub the coat to dry.

NOSE

The Pug's over-nose wrinkle can collect dirt and debris that, if left, can cause infection and sores. It should be wiped with a damp cotton pad and then dried carefully.

If the nose becomes dry and crusty, a tiny dab of petroleum jelly can be applied to help restore the moisture.

EYES

Check the eyes daily and remove any buildup of debris that may collect in the corner, using a moist cotton pad (a separate one for each eye to avoid cross-infection). Make sure no lint from the pad gets into the eye.

You should also check that the eyeball does not become dry – a problem that can occur at any time in a dog's life, but is more common in older dogs. If "dry eye" does occur, seek immediate veterinary advice, as artificial tears may need to be applied.

EARS

Pugs do tend to get dirty ears, so wipe them with a moist cotton pad regularly. Do not push into the ear, or use cotton swabs, as you could push dirt further down, and may even damage the ear. If the ear becomes red, smelly, has excess dirt, or is irritating your dog (he may scratch at his ears or shake his head), seek veterinary advice.

FEET

Check your Pug's feet daily, particularly after walks, as debris and grass seed can become

GROOMING ROUTINE

Brush the coat all over, using a soft bristle brush or a hound glove.

Clean the wrinkle over the nose, removing dirt and debris.

Clean the ears with a cotton pad, making sure you do not probe too deeply.

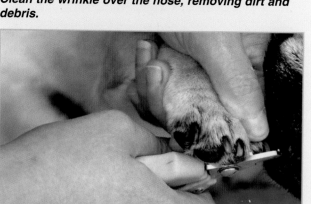

Trim the nails, using guillotine nail-clippers.

Teeth should be brushed using a canine toothpaste.

embedded in the pad, or between the toes. Also keep a lookout for interdigital cysts – sore, red lumps that weep, and that will require veterinary treatment.

NAILS

Even if you walk your Pug on hard surfaces, his nails may not wear down naturally, so they should be checked regularly. If your Pug's dewclaws were not removed, they should also be checked – if left long, they can grow around and dig into the foot, and can also cause eye damage if the Pug scratches himself or plays with other dogs.

A Pug's nails should be black, which means you will be unable to see the "quick" (the nerves and blood supply that run vertically down the center of the nail). If the quick is cut, it will bleed profusely and will be incredibly painful to the dog. Infection could also result. To avoid this, shave just a small amount off at a time, using some guillotine-type clippers.

If in doubt about how long the nails should be, or where you should cut to, ask your veterinarian to show you. Do not take any chances – Pugs are so phobic about their feet that any unpleasant experience will heighten your puppy's fear and you will have great difficulty getting anywhere near his feet in the future.

TEETH

Small breeds are renowned for their dental problems – and the Pug is no exception. It is important, therefore, to get your puppy used to having his teeth cleaned from a young age.

- Apply a pea-sized amount of special canine toothpaste (available from pet stores) to a small toothbrush or fingerbrush (that fits over the tip of your finger).
- Do not use toothpaste intended for human use – doggie varieties come in palatable meat flavors.
- Open your Pug's mouth and gently brush the teeth.
- Do not stop if your dog wants to play with the brush – just continue brushing for a couple of minutes, and then give lots of praise and a reward.
- Finish the session with a fun game.

If this becomes a daily routine, your Pug will learn to accept it. Some Pugs race into the bathroom every morning and wait to have their teeth cleaned – some even have their own brush head for an electric toothbrush!

Pug puppies usually start teething from the age of three months. His baby teeth will start to fall out and his permanent, adult teeth will grow through. During this time, your Pug is likely to gnaw more than usual, so stock up on suitable chews in preparation. You should also check the teeth regularly to ensure that the adult teeth are not growing through before the puppy teeth have fallen out – sometimes a puppy can retain his milk teeth. Seek veterinary advice if you suspect he requires professional dentistry.

OLDER DOG

Small breeds generally enjoy longer lives than their larger cousins, and Pugs are no exception.

The average life span is around 12 to 14 years, but it is not unheard of for Pugs to reach their late teens.

All dogs are individuals and age differently, but typical signs of aging are as follows:

- The coat will become gray – particularly around the muzzle – and may thin.
- Teeth may fall out (or need to be removed).
- The dog may experience joint stiffness – particularly in the back legs – which will be worse in the morning or after other periods of prolonged inactivity.

PUG PEDICURES

If your oldie exercises less, his nails will not be wearing down as before, and he may need his claws clipped more often.

- Hearing and eyesight may deteriorate.
- The dog's appetite may change. Females often put on weight, and males lose weight – though very old Pugs often become thinner and have a less hearty appetite, regardless of their sex.
- The dog will sleep more, and may want shorter walks.

Character-wise, the dog may become quieter and more sedate, and he may lose patience with younger, more boisterous dogs. He may become more loving with his owners (if this is possible!), and his day may be spent seeking nice, warm laps for quiet cuddling and a snooze.

Regular grooming to keep an eye on any lumps or changes in your dog is very important, and veterinary checkups every six months are also recommended.

DIET

Older dogs have different nutritional needs than younger ones. Because oldies are generally less active, they require fewer calories.

The composition of the food should also be different – veterans require less protein, phosphorus, and sodium, and may need larger amounts of zinc, some vitamins, essential fatty acids, and amino acids.

The veteran Pug deserves special consideration.

Breeder Kathy Newsome from Washington, Tyne and Wear, in the U.K. has owned many breeds in her life – Dachshunds, Boxers, Cockers, and German Shepherds. Although the Pug is a fraction of the size of some of these breeds, he quickly captured her heart – and has remained there ever since….

"I have owned Pugs since 1970," explains Kathy, who specializes in black coats. "They are such lovely little dogs – outgoing and cheeky. Pugs aren't like dogs at all – they are like little human beings!

"Black Pugs generally mature later than the fawns, and, in my experience, they remain more playful and lively later in life, and are often long-lived. My Stathis was a case in point – he died just six hours short of his 19th birthday!

"I bought Stathis when he was five-and-a-half weeks of age. One of my dogs sired him, and I wanted one of the puppies to breed back to my bitches, and to use as a stud dog. It all worked out very well. In the first litter that Stathis sired,

he produced a Champion.

"All my dogs have Greek names, and Stathis was no exception. He was a very loving dog and slept on the end of my bed every night – from the first day I brought him home until the day he died.

"Stathis was a lovely old fella, who used to suck on my arm like a baby. By the time he was in his high teens, he didn't have a tooth in his head, so it didn't hurt! Despite being all gums, he still wolfed back his food with no difficulty at all.

"Stathis started slowing down around the age of 13 or 14 – though he was still very much in charge of all the other dogs at that age. He was definitely top dog, and wouldn't take any nonsense from the other males. He was marvellous with all the puppies, though. He was very tolerant and gentle with them, and would curl up beside them when they slept. Stathis remained playful and mischievous right to the end, so had a lot in common with the pups!

"Stathis enjoyed sleeping more as he aged, and would laze outside in the warm sunshine. He became a little wobbly on his legs, but I used a magnetic collar, which eased his arthritis.

"One day, Stathis was enjoying a cuddle on my lap. He was dozing, and then suddenly his legs shook, and he died. There was no pain – his body was just worn out after such a long life, and he died. It was very peaceful.

"Two of Stathis's daughters are with me. Penny and Kizzy are both 15 years of age, and are healthy and eating well. Hopefully, they will follow in their daddy's pawsteps, and enjoy the same remarkable longevity."

Stathis: A gentle, tolerant dog, who remained playful until the end of his life.

Creating the ideal diet can be time-consuming and requires a great deal of specialist knowledge – it is far better to opt for a complete food that is formulated specifically for veterans. If you wish to use a homemade diet, consult your veterinarian, who will be able to advise you about exactly the types and quantities to feed and any supplements you should be giving.

If your dog loses his appetite, mix something smelly in with his usual food – some liver, fish, or a little pâté, for example. The smell should revive his interest in the food. If your dog goes 24 hours without eating, consult your veterinarian.

Because an older dog's digestion cannot cope as well as a younger dog's, you may want to consider feeding several small meals throughout the day.

Nutritional requirements change as a dog gets older.

EUTHANASIA

As a pet owner, it is your responsibility to care for your Pug's well-being, and that includes ensuring that he does not suffer unnecessarily. If your Pug becomes seriously ill, and the veterinarian advises that no further treatment can be given, you should consider your dog's quality of life. Is he in pain? Is he enjoying his food? Is he still enjoying life? If your dog is suffering, you should do some soul-searching and consider the option of euthanasia.

Euthanasia, meaning "good death" in Greek, is a painless way of ending an animal's life via an injection of barbiturates. The death is peaceful, and often looks as if the animal has just fallen asleep.

Painful as it will be for you, do not keep your Pug alive just because you cannot bear to lose him. Remember your responsibility to your dog, and show him your love by considering the best options for him.

Losing any dog is terribly upsetting, but losing a Pug is particularly difficult – they are such excellent companion dogs that it will feel as if you have lost your shadow. If you have another Pug at home, he is likely to grieve too, as Pugs bond very closely with their canine housemates. They may lose their appetite and become withdrawn.

Getting another Pug companion is often the best way of helping your Pug – and it can also help the owner, too. Giving a good home to another Pug is the best tribute you can pay to your dog.

WHAT A CHARACTER

Clownish and mischievous, Pugs are great fun to have around, but their greatest asset is their human bond. They can tune into their owners' moods and know when a comforting lap cuddle is in order. Certainly, when Sylvia Liffen from Teddington, Middlesex, U.K. was in need of a hug, devoted Pug Jacko was always there.

"Regency Lodge Crackerjack – otherwise known as Jacko – was my third Pug," explains Sylvia. "I had him from when he was 12 weeks old, and he had lots of health problems initially. He was unable to digest his food and nobody knew why. Numerous tests revealed nothing, and it wasn't until he was six months old that it was discovered he had a hiatus hernia.

"When Jacko was recovering from his operation, my husband, Roy, was recovering from treatment for prostate cancer at the same time, and they would both sit up together in bed and keep each other company. They became very close during this time."

LAST LINK

"When Roy died, Jacko was my last link with him. He pined so much for my husband that the veterinarian recommended I get another Pug to give Jacko something to focus on. The moment we got Teddy, they hit it off right away, and Jacko immediately perked up – the transformation was incredible. Pugs love the company of other dogs (particularly other Pugs), and Jacko and Teddy became good buddies almost instantly. Jacko was

Jacko: He was allowed to end his life with dignity.

six when Teddy came along, and, from being very morose and miserable, he became happy and young at heart again.

"Of course, Teddy didn't just help Jacko, he helped me too. Watching the dogs playing together in the long, dark evenings helped a great deal.

"Jacko was very affectionate to me at this time – he always had been, but now he seemed to sense my moods. When I came back from the hospital, he was there, ready to leap on my lap. He really got me through a very bad patch.

"Despite extensive early treatment as a puppy, Jacko was very close to his veterinarian. I would say to him, 'Let's go and see Dr. Monroe,' and he'd rush about with excitement. He'd run down the steps to the clinic, and wouldn't shut up in the waiting room until Dr. Monroe saw and spoke to him. 'It's not often that my patients are so pleased to see me,' Dr. Monroe would say.

"Given his early problems, I always knew that Jacko wouldn't make old bones, as my previous long-lived Pugs had done. One weekend, at the age of nine-and-a-half years, Jacko had a heart attack. He developed fluid on the lungs, had an enlarged heart, lost the use of his back legs, and wouldn't eat. Once his hernia had been corrected nine years earlier, Jacko became rather a greedy dog. When he stopped enjoying his food, I knew that something was seriously wrong. I cooked him all his favorite things, but still he refused to eat."

THE KINDEST OPTION

"There were a couple of things the veterinarian could have tried to prolong Jacko's life by a day or two, but for such a short extension, I didn't think it was fair to put him through more treatment.

"I would still have had to carry him in and out of the yard so he could go to the toilet, and, knowing what a proud little dog he was, I knew this was not what Jacko wanted. My veterinarian and I agreed that it was kinder to put Jacko to sleep.

"With dogs, you can put them out of their agony, and ensure they are not in any pain – something you cannot do for humans. It is your responsibility to make sure your dog does not suffer.

"Teddy was distraught when Jacko did not come home, and so I bought Samson, now five months old. He is a strong dog, and something of a hooligan, but full of life. He has helped us both to come to terms with Jacko's death."

CHAPTER SIX

PROBLEM BEHAVIOR

Pugs have the sweetest, most innocent of faces. Do not be fooled by the angel routine, though – Pugs can be as naughty as any other dog, sometimes more so! Pugs are loving and playful, but they can be mischievous and stubborn – and they are very good at using their large, dreamy eyes to get them out of trouble!

Early training and socialization is very important to keep a lid on the negative aspects of their personality. They should be taught, right from the start, that you are the boss – the pack leader. This is achieved through firm but fair handling, and complete consistency. Never turn a blind eye to something – if you do not allow your Pug on your bed, for example, always ask him to get off. If you let him on just once, you will encourage him to keep trying his luck.

Do not think that the hard work is over once your Pug emerges from puppyhood. Often, adolescence presents its own difficulties, and

these can continue well into the dog's adulthood if they are not corrected.

If problems persist or escalate, seek the help of an experienced trainer or behaviorist. All problems can be solved with the right approach and know-how – there's no need to put up with unsociable or irritating behavior.

SEPARATION ANXIETY

Pugs are companion dogs by name and by nature. They love being with people, and will often follow their owners from room to room around the house. This affectionate, loving nature is one of the great benefits of sharing your life with a Pug, but it can become a disadvantage if you do not prepare your dog for being able to cope during short periods without you.

If a Pug is used to your company every hour of every day, he is likely to become very distressed if you need to leave him with friends while you go on vacation, or if you have to spend some time in the hospital. Some Pugs even get upset if their owner goes shopping without them for a couple of hours!

This problem is called separation anxiety. The dog's distress at being alone can manifest itself in many ways, including:

- Repetitive barking
- Self-harm (excessive grooming/nibbling of the coat/paws – to the point of causing sores to the skin)
- Destructive behavior (e.g. destroying furniture and furnishings by scratching at doors to be with the owner, chewing the doors, ripping up the sofa, and so forth)
- Lapses in house-training (see page 46)
- Anxiety – often resulting in the dog becoming increasingly possessive of the owner.

The Pug is such a people-dog, he may become stressed if he has to cope on his own.

Prevention

It is important to get the puppy used to being on his own for short periods from a young age. No dog should be left for hours on end, of course. Once the puppy has been introduced to the crate and is happy to be inside it (see page 31), place him inside for 20 minutes, three or four times a day. Don't make a big fuss over him immediately before or immediately after he is in the crate.

As the puppy gets older, extend the length of time he is inside – for example, an hour twice a day. If his crate sessions are a regular part of his routine, he will soon settle inside it and have a snooze. Leave a safe chew-toy inside the crate so that he can amuse himself if he doesn't want a nap.

Never return to the dog if he barks. To do so would teach him that, when he calls, you come running. Wait for him to stop barking, or distract him so he stops. Then let him out.

Trouble-shooting

If your Pug develops separation anxiety, there are a number of measures you can take to deal with the problem.

Stair-gate

- Place a stair-gate across the doorway between two rooms.
- Put your Pug on the other side of the gate from you for short periods, several times a day.
- Give him a distraction, such as a chew-toy, so he doesn't get bored.

If you use a stair-gate, you can still be seen, but your Pug is learning to be left on his own.

- The gate will help him to get used to being in a different room from you, while giving him the security that you are still close by and within sight.
- Gradually increase the time that your dog is behind the gate. Start with just five minutes; when he is relaxed and can cope with this period, increase it to ten, then 15 and so on.

Crate

- Get your dog used to being in his crate (see page 31).
- When he is comfortable being inside it, get into the habit of using it several times a day.
- Place him inside, while you dust, polish, do the dishes, and so forth. Act normally – if you make it seem like a big deal, your Pug will detect your anxiety and become nervous.
- As your Pug gets used to being inside his crate, walk out of the room and immediately back again. As before, act normally.

- Over several sessions, increase the length of time you are out of the room – five seconds to 10 seconds, 15 seconds and so on.
- When your dog is fine with you being out of the room for 10 minutes or so, then introduce your "leaving cue." Many separation anxiety dogs begin to get distressed before their owner leaves. They have learned that a departure is preceded by a set routine – the owner putting on his shoes, fetching a coat, and picking up his keys.

Work at crate-training your Pug, so he feels safe and secure in his own personal "den."

- Now, when your dog is in his crate and is enjoying "time-out" from your company, put your shoes on and then continue as usual – read the paper, make a phone call, and so forth.
- Walk out of the room for just a second or two, before returning to the room.
- Put your shoes on and off throughout the day, and keep doing this so it stops being a cue to your going out.
- Do the same with putting your coat on, picking your keys up, or other actions.
- If your dog cries or barks at any of these cues, do not react. Remain calm and ignore his excitement. Continue to act as if everything is perfectly normal.
- Over the course of many weeks, get your dog used to you opening the front door. Return to the room he is in right away. As before, gradually extend the length of time between opening the front door and returning to the room.
- Next, practice closing the door after you, and then returning to the house.
- Now, start your car engine for just a few seconds before returning indoors.
- The retraining should be slow and steady – don't rush any of the exercises, and don't move forward a step before your dog has mastered the stage he is at.

BARKING

Pugs are not yappy little Toy dogs, but they do like to have their say on certain matters. For example, if they feel that the postman or window cleaner poses a real threat to their household security, they will not rest until they have seen the intruder off. In their eyes, the intruder disappears because of the barking – not because they have finished their job and were leaving anyway! Pugs are big dogs trapped in a small dog's body – they are scared of no one, and are convinced that others view them as forces to be reckoned with too!

Having a dog that gives a warning bark can be a useful deterrent to would-be burglars (without seeing your dog, no one would ever suspect that the Pug's bark belonged to a Toy dog). However, if the barking is becoming a nuisance and extends to barking at anything and everything, you should start some serious training together before you are driven to distraction!

If your Pug gets overexcited and barks excessively, try diverting his attention with a toy or a treat.

First, it is important to reeducate your Pug about people who approach the house. For example, pre-empt the behavior by distracting your dog with a different rewarding activity when the postman arrives. If your Pug is busy doing some basic obedience exercises, and is receiving treats in the process, he will be focused on you rather than the perceived intruder. He will also begin to associate the postman's arrival with a rewarding experience – once this link has been made, he will welcome his approach, not try to chase him away.

About 10 minutes before you anticipate the postman's arrival, practice some obedience exercises or play a game together in the yard, as far away from the front door as possible. Over a period of several weeks, gradually move closer to the house. The next step is to train in a room in the house that is farthest from the front door, and gradually move closer to the front door.

Invite some visitors to the house and hand them treats to give to your Pug. If he barks when they enter the house, the dog should be ignored. When he is quiet and well behaved, then he can be given attention and a treat.

If your dog barks at any time, distract him. Show him a tastier treat, bring out a new toy to play with – anything to get him focused on you.

Never shout at the dog for barking – in his eyes, you will be joining in with his barking, Your Pug will feel that you are upset at the intruder too, and will bark especially vigorously to make the person go away and stop upsetting his owner!

The Pug has a famous stubborn streak, and can become too fond of getting his own way.

STUBBORNNESS

Pugs are happy, loving animals, but some can exhibit stubborn streaks. They are renowned for their love of home comforts, and can be particularly obstinate when it comes to these – Pugs enjoy the high life!

Some do not take kindly to being refused access to the bed. Others will get grumpy if they cannot snooze on the sofa. Where you allow your dog to rest is immaterial – the important thing is that your Pug respects you. He must get off the sofa or bed as soon as you ask him to – no questions asked. No grumbles, no growling, and certainly no snapping. A dog that respects the pack leader would not hesitate to obey such a command – if your dog does put up a fight, it's time to reassess your relationship and to start being the boss again.

This doesn't mean that you should start throwing your weight around, bellowing at every opportunity and behaving like a tyrant. Bullies don't make good leaders – or owners. Instead, you should provide stable, consistent leadership through firm, fair handling. Dogs like hierarchy – they don't even mind being bottom of the pack, as long as they know their role.

- Set out the house rules, and make sure that all family members are clear about what is permitted, and that they agree to uphold the rules.
- Never let your dog get away with breaking the rules. If your Pug is not allowed on the sofa and you find him on it, ask him to get off.
- If your dog doesn't get off when you ask him, pick him up and remove him – then work on his general obedience! (See Chapter Four.)

If your dog is being stubborn and you need to remind him who's boss, try the following:

- Eat your meals before feeding him.
- Walk through doorways ahead of him.
- Walk ahead of him on stairs.
- Groom him regularly.
- Do not let him on your bed or your favorite chair.

These measures may sound petty, but, to a dog, they would be significant signals of his inferior status in the pack. Eating first, having the best bed/resting area, etc. are all privileges exclusive to the top dog – you! It is also important to train your dog regularly. It will improve your relationship, and your Pug will learn that obeying you is rewarding and fun.

If your dog persists in being stubborn and attempts to bite you, or anyone else, ask your veterinarian to refer you to a reputable behavior counsellor.

HOUSE-TRAINING LAPSES

A Pug's house-training can lapse at any time. First, you should get the dog checked by a veterinarian, as there may be a health reason for his change in behavior.

If no medical problem is responsible, then you must go back to the drawing board and train your Pug all over again (see page 46). Take him outside frequently, as you would a puppy; indoors, be vigilant to the warning signs that indicate he needs to relieve himself (page 47).

You must also get to the root cause as to why your dog's house-training has lapsed. Consider if any patterns emerge. For example, one common reason for a breakdown in house-training is poor weather.

In cold, wet, or windy weather, your luxury-loving Pug may decide he doesn't want to go outside, and so will relieve himself in the warm comfort of his own home. Is there a porch or other sheltered area outdoors that you could take him to? If not, invest in a fleecy coat (for him and you!), and a large fishing umbrella that will cover him completely.

Give extra-special treats when he performs outside in cold weather to make it all worth his

Think long and hard before making the decision to neuter your Pug.

while. Do not throw him outside and leave him to it while you enjoy a cup of coffee inside – he will just try to get inside and will not perform. Instead, stay outside with him – solidarity is vital!

Dogs are tempted to relieve themselves in places where they have done so before, so clean up his accidents thoroughly to discourage him from returning to the scene of the crime.

Remember that most household cleaners will not remove all the scent (a dog's sense of smell is infinitely superior to our own). Use a proprietary brand designed specifically to deal with accidents, or a solution of biological cleaning powder. Do not use any ammonia-based cleaner – to a dog's nose this will smell very similar to urine, and may actually encourage him to continue to use the spot.

DOMINANCE/SUBMISSION

Sometimes, dogs urinate to exert their dominance (territorial marking). It can often be cured through castration, but, by then, the behavior may have become habitual so this is not always a reliable solution.

Conversely, dogs can also urinate to indicate their submission (in such cases, they are likely to squat, rather than lift a leg). A nervous puppy may wee when he meets someone new or scary to show that he is not a threat. In either instance, advice should be sought from a qualified veterinary behaviorist.

NEUTERING

Sometimes hormones are the cause of behavioral problems (such as scent-marking). If your veterinarian advises that this is the case with your Pug, neutering may be recommended.

Neutering is also beneficial to your pet's health. In females, removing the uterus also removes any chance of pyometra (a life-threatening uterine infection), and dramatically reduces the chance of your female Pug developing mammary tumors.

Some pet owners prefer not to contend with seasons too, and all the complications of trying to keep her away from other dogs during this time. Plus, there will be no chance of being presented with an unwanted (possibly crossbred) litter. If your female does become pregnant, not only will you be burdened with the cost (which can be very high if a caesarean is required, or if there are other complications with the birth), but you will also have to keep any puppies for whom you are unable to find decent homes.

In male dogs, castration removes the possibility of prostate and testicular disorders, and should prevent the dog from marking his territory and trying to roam after females.

The decision to neuter your Pug should not be taken lightly, however. Although spaying (females) and neutering (males) are quite routine operations, they are still major surgical procedures (particularly spaying). With any surgery, there is a risk – especially when a flat-faced breed has to undergo anesthetic. Plus, there are some possible side effects after surgery:

- Weight increase (the dog may become a little less active, and this may result in a weight increase. It is easily solved: just adjust your dog's diet accordingly – see page 56).
- Incontinence in females (though some contend that this can occur in older unspayed Pugs anyway and may not be linked to neutering).

When to neuter is a controversial point. Some veterinarians recommend performing the operation before sexual maturity. Others prefer to wait until after the dog has developed (i.e. not earlier than six months of age).

Generally, it is recommended that puppies should not be neutered until after they have reached sexual maturity.

Discuss any concerns you have with your veterinarian, who will help to guide you to the right decision given your own individual circumstances.

CHAPTER SEVEN

THE VERSATILE PUG

With his snub nose and small size, the Pug is not the first breed that springs to mind when thinking of dog sports such as Agility. However, this is a lively, intelligent breed, with a great deal to offer the owner interested in doing more with their canine companion.

The range of canine hobbies is extensive and there is something to suit almost everyone, depending on personal preferences, the dog's age and fitness, and the time you can devote to your chosen sport. Whether you want to show your Pug or experience the thrill of racing round an agility course, this chapter will introduce you to the many activities you can enjoy together.

CANINE GOOD CITIZEN

The "Good Citizen" scheme is an excellent starting point for anyone wishing to further their Pug's initial puppy training and socialization. In the U.K., the Good Citizen Dog Scheme is run by the Kennel Club, while, in the U.S., the Canine Good Citizen Program is run by the American Kennel Club. To receive his Good Citizen award, your dog will need to demonstrate that he can behave appropriately in a variety of everyday situations, including:

- Accepting handling and grooming
- Responding to basic obedience commands
- Meeting another dog
- Walking on a loose leash in a controlled manner
- Walking confidently through a crowd of people
- Being approached and petted by a stranger.

By enrolling at one of the many Good Citizen training clubs located throughout the U.K. and the U.S., you will be taught how to prepare yourself and your dog for the tests. To find out more, contact your national kennel club.

OBEDIENCE

If you enjoyed training your Pug as a puppy, you may like to try Competitive Obedience trials – one of the few sports available to Pugs in which their physical limitations do not have a detrimental effect on their performance. As our case study shows, Pugs can rise to the very top.

If you think Competitive Obedience may be just the thing for you and your Pug, you will need to join an Obedience training club. Your national kennel club will be able to provide you with details of clubs in your area. In the meantime, the following exercise will give you a taste of what is involved.

AGILITY

Agility is best described as an obstacle course for dogs. Each dog must successfully negotiate a series of obstacles within a set time and with no faults. The winner is the dog that has the fastest time with the fewest mistakes.

Agility requires a fair amount of physical fitness, so you will need to ensure that you and your dog are fit and healthy. You should also be aware of age restrictions. This is because the demanding nature of some of the obstacles can cause damage to the joints of a puppy or a dog still growing. Your national kennel club will tell you what age restrictions apply in your country.

A MERRY DOG

Pamela Dawe's interest in Obedience began when she acquired her first Pug, Merry. "Merry adored basic Obedience, and would squeal with delight when we arrived at the classes. She loved it so much, I decided to try some advanced Obedience."

Merry's biggest achievement came when she won an Obedience competition at the South Eastern Counties Toy Dog Show at Brunel University. As a result of this, she was awarded the Sebastian Cup for being the best dog in her class. The occasion was the talk of the breed ring for some time.

Sadly, Merry has now passed away, although she lived to the grand old age of 16. Until the last few months of her life, she was still competing in Obedience, such was her love of the sport. Pamela is now training her second Pug, Alice.

Pamela Dawe with (left to right) Josie, Alice, and Merry.

Christine Dresser from Medina, Ohio, is the proud owner of Ch. Webb's Neu Prize Fighter (Dempsey), the first – and, to date, only – Pug to achieve his Utility Dog Excellent (UDX) title.

"I have always enjoyed training dogs, and my interest in Obedience began in 1966, when my Whippet achieved his first Obedience title. However, I did not begin competing with Pugs until some years later.

"My first Pug was called Boo Boo Legs (full name Ch. Broughcastle Bootlegger), and he made me fall in love with the breed – we seemed to have a special connection. When I got my first black Pug, Beemus (Ch. Harper's As I Be, CD), I decided to try Obedience, and she was my first Pug to get an Obedience title.

"Training Pugs was very easy for me, because I had experience and also because Pugs are extremely eager to please and very food motivated. With encouragement and treats, you can train them to do anything! I was also fortunate to receive help and advice from two of the top Obedience trainers in my country, Mike and Linda MacDonald. They showed me just what can be achieved, even with Pugs – a breed that few people would think of when it comes to top-level Obedience.

"However, that said, there are certain precautions you need to take when training Pugs. Repeated jumping can be tough on their musculo-skeletal system, and their short muzzles affect their breathing."

MEETING THE CHALLENGE

"I am careful to avoid working in high heat and humidity, and I avoid shows held under these sorts of conditions. In addition, Pugs can develop corneal problems, which can compromise their sight. Consequently, advanced distance work in Obedience can be quite difficult. You need to take all these factors into account when you train Pugs.

"I have now trained many Pugs, and five of them have achieved Obedience titles, including three who achieved their UDs (Utility Dog titles). It is difficult to say what the breed's strengths and weaknesses are, as I've found that each dog is different. For example, Bumble Bee (Ch. Dress Circle Goldtone Glory B, UD) picked up scent discrimination within a few weeks, but Dustin took well over a year. Each Pug presents new challenges, and working

Christine Dresser with her competition Pugs.

Webb's Neu Pride Fighter UDX (Dempsey) clears the hurdles.

tremendous amount of work, but well worth it. All the training allows you to develop a remarkable rapport with your dog. I have enjoyed every minute of training my Pugs. Certainly, there are more 'traditional' Obedience breeds, but Pugs have more than proven that they can run with the big boys, and you certainly draw a crowd when you compete with a Pug amid all those Golden Retrievers, German Shepherds, and Border Collies.

"I'd recommend it to anyone – Obedience training is fun for dog and owner alike, and you will end up with an impeccably behaved companion, and, perhaps, some ribbons along the way."

through those challenges is all part of the fun.

"My greatest achievement in Obedience came when my Pug Dempsey achieved his UDX title in 2000. That year, he was also tied as the number one Obedience Pug in the country. I am particularly proud that, as well as achieving his Obedience titles, he is a breed Champion, a specialty winner, a group winner, and a sire of winning puppies. I have recently started training his granddaughter, Pearl (Ch. Trump's Dress Circle Stardust), who has so much spirit and drive she can hardly contain herself. I have high hopes for her.

"One of the joys of owning Pugs is the great character they display, although this can also prove to be frustrating. For example, Dempsey once failed Open Obedience. He was asked to perform a Drop on the Recall, and, as usual, he came running straight toward me, obedient as ever. However, instead of dropping into the Down position halfway across the ring, he bowed down his front end and left his rear end wagging in the air! It was disappointing to fail, but you don't own Pugs unless you have a sense of humor.

"In the future, I would love to achieve another UDX title with a Pug. It is a

Dempsey performs a perfect dumbbell retrieve.

Stephanie Clinesmith, from Dodge City, Kansas, was one of the first Americans to take up Agility. Today, she is a licensed judge, with many years of experience and success under her belt.

"My first Pug was Shelly (Shelly Marie Clinesmith CDX), who was responsible for my falling in love with the breed. Like most Pugs, she has the cute 'smashed' face, a wonderful personality, and seems to love everybody. Shelly is now 13 years old, and, in addition to her, I have another eight Agility Pugs.

"I took up Agility in 1992, shortly after the National Club for Dog Agility was formed (since acquired by United Kennel Club, or UKC). My local training club became licensed to hold Agility events, and that's how I became involved. From the start, I found Pugs very easy to train – they will do anything for treats!

"Agility is an unusual sport for Pugs, but they take to it very well. As long as the dog is fit, healthy, and properly built, their small size does not pose as many problems as you first may think. However, because Agility is such a physically demanding sport, it is essential that you train on the proper equipment and with proper tuition, so that you don't overstretch your Pug and cause him an injury.

"Also, some Pugs can have breathing difficulties, because they are brachycephalic (short-nosed), and, if you want to take up Agility, you need to ensure that your Pug does not suffer from this complaint. The unique physical characteristics that affect a Pug's breathing are still influencing factors even for healthy dogs – they cannot be expected to train or perform in hot weather, which can prove rather limiting. I have competed in a few outdoor Agility events, where, despite my best attempts to keep my Pugs cool, the heat overcame the dogs and they gave out halfway around the course. However, climate aside, there is no reason why a healthy Pug cannot perform really well in Agility.

U-ACH Ch. Dust Storm's Sierra Desert CD, OA, NAJ (Sierra): A Pug that needs little motivation.
Russ Burdick Photography.

DIFFERENT ATTITUDES

"Of my eight Agility Pugs, some perform much better than others, although this is usually a matter of attitude. For example, Sierra (U-ACH Ch. Dust Storm's Sierra Desert CD, OA, NAJ) is totally reliable when she runs an Agility course. I never have to motivate her, she simply has a blast and listens to everything I tell her. Baby (U-AGII Dust Storm's Baby Twister CD, NAJ), on the other hand, does not like Agility all that much, and really wishes I would let her retire. It's not that she doesn't want to please me, Agility just isn't really her thing.

"Also, some of my Pugs had problems with the A-frame, while others seemed to fly over it, which goes to show that each dog is an individual first, and a particular breed second. There are no generalizations that are true for all Pugs.

"My three main stars are Sierra, Spike (U-ACHX Spike Lee Clinesmith CDX, NA), and Tumble (U-ACHX Ch. Dust Storm Dancin' Tumbleweed CD, NA, NAJ). Spike and Tumble have each achieved UKC Agility Champion Excellent (U-ACHX) titles, while Sierra has been awarded her American Kennel Club (AKC) Open

Agility (OA) title. I have also earned several UKC High Combined Scores, which means that my dogs had the best combined scores in Agility I and II (U-AGI and U-AGII).

"Although Tumble performs really well in Agility, and she has earned her U-ACHX, her very first competition did not go well. It was, however, very memorable. We were at the start line, waiting to begin, when I gave the command 'Go!' Instead of racing off to the first obstacle, she turned around and crawled off in the opposite direction! I think her nerves overcame her, but she seems to have put all that behind her.

"On another occasion, I was really embarrassed by Storm (U-AGII Ch. Dust Storm's Eye of the Storm CD, NA, NAJ). Storm is really good at Agility, but only when he wants to be. If he is upset with me for any reason, he refuses to perform. At this one competition, he stood there and refused to budge. When we eventually made it to the first obstacle, he walked right past it, turned around, and stared at me pointedly. I ran him six times in that competition, and he refused to co-operate every time. The crowd thought it was hilarious.

U-ACHX Ch. Dust Storm Dancin' Tumbleweed CD, NA, NAJ: Working well after a nervous start. Russ Burdick Photography.

"The reason Storm was so annoyed with me was because I made him sleep in a crate, instead of sleeping with me like he usually does (the motor home I stayed in was not as cool as Pugs prefer). He was further incensed by the fact that I wouldn't let him jump up on me because the ground was so wet and muddy. Storm lives up to the generalization that Pugs can be stubborn, but this has more to do with his particular personality than the fact he is a Pug. Normally, he loves Agility, giving 100 percent effort.

"In the future, I plan to compete with my three-month-old puppy, Dust Storm's Whispering Wind. She is the daughter of Sierra, and I am hoping she has inherited some of her mother's Agility ability. She has already started training the tunnels. However, I can't teach her too much just yet as she is still growing, and she could damage her joints if she were to tackle the jumps or contact obstacles.

"I also hope that Storm and Sierra will earn their AKC Agility Excellent titles. Both are easily good enough, but it is a question of time. My main ambition is to have fun – when the fun stops, it's time to quit."

U-AGII Ch. Dust Storm's Eye of the Storm CD, NA, NAJ: A brilliant performer – when he wants to be...
Photo: Ardell Equine & Animal.

FREESTYLE

Canine Freestyle, or Heelwork to Music, is a form of Obedience set to music. At the most advanced level, Freestyle performances can be seen at shows such as Crufts in the U.K. or Westminster in the U.S., performed by accomplished artistes and trainers.

Most performances are timed to last less than five minutes, and judges award marks for two areas of the performance:

- **Technical:** this assesses accuracy, the synchronization between dog and owner, and the degree of difficulty in the routine.
- **Presentation:** this covers costume and the artistic flair shown in the choreography. You need to reach a reasonable standard of basic obedience before getting started.

If you are interested in taking up Freestyle, contact your national kennel club for more information on how to get involved.

DANCING WITH NEWMAN

Mari Beth Baumberger, from South Dakota, acquired her first Pug, a rescue puppy called Newman, seven years ago.

"Newman was born with luxating patellas (a problem with his kneecaps). His breeder did not want him, so he ended up with me. I didn't know anything about Pugs when he came to me, but, having owned Newman for the last seven years, I would say that his friendly, entertaining attitude and his affection are what make Pugs irresistible to so many people.

"As soon as I could, I took Newman to pet obedience classes. He did really well and my instructor told me that I was a natural trainer. I decided to take up Freestyle after seeing a video of Sandra Davis and her dogs. I thought it was great and decided to start teaching Newman some basic moves. Newman loved it, really putting his whole personality into it.

"I enjoyed Freestyle from the

Mari Beth Baumberger and Newman, dancing with style.

beginning, because not only do I love to train dogs, but I also love music, dancing, and entertaining, and Freestyle combines them all. It gives me a chance to showcase Newman's talent and the bond we share, for all sorts of audiences to enjoy.

"Like all the other activities that Newman and I trained for, I found that Newman's motivation was strongest if we didn't train for too long, so our motto was quality not quantity. I also found that he liked certain moves more than others, such as spins, so I tried to throw in a few of these in each session, to keep his interest.

"Pugs are probably not the first breed you would think of when you think of Freestyle, but their entertaining character really seems to endear them to audiences, and their physical characteristics mean that, when they execute a move, they make it truly their own. Seeing a Pug perform a dance routine is really quite special."

CARTING

Although the British and American Kennel Clubs have yet to recognize Carting as an affiliated sport, many breeds of dog and their owners enjoy this unusual activity.

The sport is much more popular in America – there are no known Carting Pugs in the U.K.

Carting is seen mainly at parades and demonstrations, where it is always a crowd-puller.

Carting involves harnessing the dog to a special dog-sized cart, in a similar fashion to the horse-drawn cart. The wrong sort of cart, improperly loaded and harnessed, can cause severe damage to your Pug, so, if Carting appeals to you, enlist the help of an expert, not only to help you choose the right cart for your pet but also to show you how to train your dog correctly.

Your national club or breed club should be able to provide you with details of clubs or enthusiasts in your area.

SHOWING

Exhibiting your Pug can be great fun. For respected breeders, who have worked long and hard to produce dogs of the highest quality, showing is a chance to gain recognition for what they have achieved. However, many pet owners also enter because they enjoy the showing experience.

Competition in the show ring is fierce, and, for this reason, you will need a dog of very high quality if you intend to compete seriously. Your Pug will be measured against the Breed Standard (a "blueprint" of the ideal dog) laid down by your national kennel club (a summary is presented in Chapter Nine). Study this carefully and see if your Pug has got what it takes.

All kennel clubs require a dog to be fully registered (so that he is of proven purebred pedigree) before he can compete seriously in shows. You should make sure you receive your dog's registration papers and pedigree when you buy the puppy.

A loving pet owner will probably consider their Pug to be the best dog in the world, but most will probably find that their dog falls short of the standard required.

This is because many breeders will not sell a show-quality puppy to a pet owner, unless that owner has expressed an intention to show. In many cases, an enthusiastic pet owner goes on to acquire a new puppy, who they hope has the potential to succeed all the way to the top.

Getting Started

If you want to become involved in showing, the first step is to enroll at ring-training classes. These will teach you how to perform in the show ring and how to present your pet to the best advantage.

For details of training clubs in your area, contact your veterinary hospital or pet store.

Types of Shows

Most dog shows categorize the dogs according to group. In the U.K. and the U.S., the Pug is placed in the Toy group.

EOAN'S CART

Judith A. Daly, from Massachusetts, is the owner of Ch. Kendoric's Leprechaun in Black CD, otherwise known as Eoan (pronounced Owen), an eight-year-old Pug who adores Carting.

"In 1992, I got my first Pug. He was supposed to be a present for my husband, but I fell in love with the breed and have kept Pugs ever since. Eoan came along two years later, as an eight-week-old puppy.

"I got into Carting by accident. I was taking Eoan to Obedience and handling classes at a kennel that bred Rottweilers and German Shepherds. Eoan was the only small dog there, and the other class members would frequently tease me about getting a 'real' dog. One Sunday, the club hosted a seminar on Carting, and everyone thought it was a huge joke that I came along with my Pug – until we got there and Eoan put a stop to everyone's comments.

"I came to the seminar with a plastic toy cart and a makeshift harness I had adapted from an adjustable one bought from a pet store. When you teach a dog to cart, you don't hitch him up to the cart right away. You start by putting on the harness and letting the dog get used to that. Then you attach a metal bar to the harness and get the dog used to pulling the bar, and, eventually, you progress to the cart. Eoan got through the entire process in one day and amazed everyone – including me! I had to go out and buy him a real cart and have a special harness custom-made for him.

"Eoan adores Carting. When I pull out his cart he starts dancing around. He gets so excited I have difficulty getting him hitched up. Eoan is a natural-born show-off, and he thinks it's the greatest thing to strut around and get so much attention. At his first public appearance with a cart, he stopped the events in all the rings around him.

"Since then, he's done several demonstrations, including two national Specialty shows. One of his most memorable demonstrations was at Christmas. He did a two-mile parade carting a small bear and a Christmas tree with real lights on it. On another occasion, at our Patriot Pug Dog Club 2001 Specialty Show, he delivered the judges' presents in his carts. It was a real show-stopper!

"I firmly believe that, if Carting titles were available, Eoan would have achieved them all, he's such a natural at the sport. His small size hasn't limited him in any way. Obviously, I had to buy smaller, Pug-size equipment for him, but most Carting supply companies already have these in stock – Carting is becoming increasingly popular among all breeds."

Eoan giving puppy rides at the PDCA National at Wisconsin.

A CLEAN SWEEP

Becky Willis, from Cheshire in the U.K. has always owned pet Pugs, but, until recently, her showing experience was limited to horses, which she bred. After entering a few dog shows for fun, Becky has now decided to take up the sport of showing in earnest…

"I got into the world of dog showing when my sister entered her Pug in a show hosted by the Pug Dog Club. She didn't expect to do particularly well, but on her first show her Pug qualified for a place at Crufts! After that, we both decided to enter a few more shows.

"I had some experience of the show environment from exhibiting my horses, and I found that showing dogs was easier. As long as you own a well-behaved, well-socialized dog, it is not too difficult. However, I did need to attend ring-training classes, so that I could learn how to present my dogs to their best advantage. Pugs are table dogs, which means that the judge assesses their physical conformation while the dog is standing on a table, and ring-training classes showed me how to teach my dogs to stand correctly.

"When I first started dog showing, it was purely for fun, but, after one of my pet Pugs died, I decided to go for a Pug that would, hopefully, be good enough to do well in the show ring. I got Sweep (Sheffawn Chimney Sweep) as an adorable little black puppy. He didn't do particularly well in his first few shows, as he was a slightly underdeveloped puppy. However, he always managed to get placed, and he has matured into a very handsome adult, now three years old.

"Probably my proudest moment with him came at his first appearance at Crufts, two years ago. At his first appearance, he came second in his class – a major achievement for a novice like me.

"I now have another show Pug, Poppy (Marbelton Busy Busy Bee). She is a delightful, seven-month-old fawn puppy. I hope that she will go on to be my first Pug to win a Challenge Certificate, and, if she is successful, I would like to begin a breeding program, using her as my foundation female.

"My advice to anyone else thinking of becoming involved in showing, is go for it! It's a really fun, sociable activity, and Pug people are extremely friendly. Anyone who begins showing Pugs will be given a great deal of support from them."

Becky Willis with (pictured, left to right) Marbelton Busy Busy Bee (Poppy), and Sheffawn Chimney Sweep (Sweep).

U.K. Shows

There are a number of informal shows held throughout the country by various organizations, but the main shows are known as Limited, Open, or Championship shows.

- **Limited shows:** these can be entered only by members of the organization hosting the show. Usually, different breeds within the same group (e.g. all the breeds in the Toy group) compete against each other in so-called "any variety" classes.
- **Open shows:** as the name suggests, these are open to all. Open shows contain breed classes as well as "any variety" classes.
- **Championship shows:** these are the biggest and most important shows, with classes divided into breeds. For each breed there are two Challenge Certificates (CCs) available, one for the best bitch and one for the best dog.

  At the end of all the breed classes, the two CC winners are entered into a final class to compete for Best of Breed (BOB).

  Any dog or bitch that wins three CCs under three different judges becomes a Show Champion.

U.S. Shows

Like the U.K., there are a number of informal or "match" shows held, but to make your dog a Champion, you would need to compete in a series of "licensed" or "point" shows, where Championship points are on offer. There are two types of licensed shows:

- **Specialty shows:** specific breeds of dog, or groupings of breeds, can compete against each other in these shows (e.g. Pugs only, or a mixture of different Toy breeds).
- **All breed shows:** These are similar to Championship shows in the U.K. (see opposite), with classes divided into breeds, and winners chosen from each class.

  The winners of each breed are entered into a Group competition, and the winners from the Group competitions are entered into a final contest to win the title of Best in Show.

  The maximum number of points a dog can earn in any one show is five, and Champions are made by earning a total of 15 points.

  The 15 points need to include two "majors" (three-, four-, or five-point awards), awarded by separate judges.

SUCCESS AND FAILURE

At your first show it is unlikely that you will do particularly well. Do not let this dishearten you – few people achieve outstanding results when they first start off. Your dog's performance and your handling skills will improve with time and experience, thereby improving your chances of success.

Always remember, however, that you should love your pet unconditionally. It is certainly not his fault if he falls a little short of the expected standard.

You should love him unreservedly and, win or lose, you know you have the best dog in the world.

SHOW RING HEAVEN

Danielle M. Campi, of Northern California, was always fascinated with the world of dog shows, even before her aunt and uncle took her to the Golden Gate Kennel Club dog show when she was a very small child. As long as she can remember, it was her lifelong goal to breed and exhibit top-quality dogs. She just didn't know what breed until she met her first Pug.

In 1996, Danielle acquired her first show Pug, a two-year-old fawn female who became Ch. Larimar's Stardust CD, CGC, ROM. Star was Danielle's first Pug to be made an owner-handled conformation Champion, an Obedience title holder, a Canine Good Citizen, and a Register of Merit dam.

As well as being a much-loved pet, Star became the foundation matron for Danielle's successful Celestial Pugs. To date, she has owner-handled four Champions, two from her own breeding program. In the five litters that Danielle has bred or cobred since 1998, there are six Champions and twelve other show-prospect Pugs working on further show ring success throughout the United States.

Ch. Larimar's Stardust CD, CGC, ROM (pictured center with Danielle M. Campi, with her six-month-old puppies Am. Can. Ch. Celestial Neu Star Premiere (left), and Celestial Neu Star Debut (right).

CHAPTER EIGHT

A SPECIAL BOND

The Pug was bred as a companion dog, and, because of this, many people make the mistake of assuming that he is suited to nothing more than a life of idle companionship. However, the Pug is an intelligent, lively breed, that benefits a great deal from "extracurricular" activities.

As well as the canine sports described in chapter seven, there are several working avenues available that really make the most of the Pug's affectionate and spirited disposition. Many people think of Golden Retrievers or Labradors when they think of dogs that help the disabled, but there is no reason why Pugs cannot do just as good a job. Dogs for the disabled, blind, or deaf, however, are trained from puppyhood, and are specially chosen as puppies, but, if this sort of work appeals to you, and you think your Pug would enjoy the experience, why not become involved with therapy work, bringing joy to those who would otherwise have no contact with animals?

This chapter aims to show how Pugs throughout the world are involved in assistance and therapy work, as well as giving you tips on how to become involved.

ASSISTANCE DOGS

There are several types of assistance dogs, working with a variety of people – from the blind and the deaf to those who are disabled or handicapped.

The dog's role is to fill the gaps created by the owner's disability, whether that is barking to alert a deaf owner that the doorbell has just rung, or helping a handicapped person to put on their socks.

Due to the Pug's physical characteristics, and the dominance of breeds such as the Golden Retriever, there are relatively few Pugs working as assistance dogs. However, this is not to say that the breed is unsuitable for assistance work, as the following case history shows.

MAGICAL MYRTLE

Jonathan Purchase, from Plymouth in the U.K. has recently acquired his first Hearing Dog, Myrtle. Here, he describes the impact Myrtle has had on his life.

"I began developing hearing problems about eight years ago, and it has become progressively worse ever since. I now have 95 percent loss in my right ear, and 50 percent loss in my left. I am unable to understand people's speech unless I lip-read, and I cannot hear many everyday sounds, such as telephones and doorbells.

"My hearing problem is one that cannot be cured, and, when I was first diagnosed and given a prognosis, I became quite depressed. Hearing loss makes you feel very isolated, so the effect is a psychological one as much as a physical one. I knew I had to come to terms with my problem and learn to live with it, although that is, of course, far easier said than done.

"It was my hearing therapist who suggested I apply for a Hearing Dog. I had never owned a dog of any breed before, and didn't know about Hearing Dogs. My therapist explained that the dogs help with everyday sounds a person needs to be aware of, such as doorbells, telephones, alarm clocks, and smoke alarms. I decided to apply for a dog, and, three months later, I was visited at home to see if I was suitable. After another two years, I was offered Myrtle. I didn't have a preference for a particular breed of dog, but, as soon as I saw a photo of Myrtle, I knew she was the dog for me.

"I was invited to stay at the Hearing Dog Center, along with my wife and children, for a week of intensive training with Myrtle. The staff were wonderful, very patient and truly understanding of the difficulties facing someone with a hearing impairment. After a week's training, I was allowed to take Myrtle home.

"Myrtle has been with me for only six weeks, but my life has already changed because of her. To begin with, I have lost a few pounds from the extra exercise that dog ownership forces upon you! The first thing she does, every day, is to wake me when my alarm clock goes off. She

Jonathan with his son, Josh, and Hearing Dog Myrtle.

does this by jumping on the bed and pawing me. My wife used to wake me by elbowing me in the ribs, so I think I prefer Myrtle's more gentle approach!

"Myrtle also lets me know when the telephone is ringing, or when someone has rung the doorbell. When my wife is at work I used to rely on the children for this, but, being children, they frequently forgot. Myrtle never does. She has also improved my working life. People at work have been great, and they got me a vibrating pager so that I could be aware of fire alarms and public address messages, but a pager cannot tell me if someone is calling me from across the room. If Myrtle hears someone call me, she gets up and takes me to the caller. It's little things like this that make all the difference.

"Whenever I go out, Myrtle comes with me. We often get looks of admiration when I take her into shops, and people often ask about her. Myrtle wears the Hearing Dog yellow jacket, and, because people see this, they realize I am deaf. Consequently, they speak more clearly and slowly, and look directly at me, which really helps my lip-reading. I am beginning to be involved in everyday conversation again, and the effect this had had on my confidence is huge.

"Myrtle is my constant companion. Everywhere I go, she goes – work, shops, restaurants, everywhere. Most people are amazed at how devoted she seems. For my part, I am devoted to her. She has transformed my life. Before I had Myrtle, I used to wake up very early, because I worried about missing the alarm clock. Now I get a much better night's sleep, because I know I don't have to worry about not hearing it – I know Myrtle will.

"Now that I have experienced life with Myrtle, I could not be without her. I would advise anyone with a hearing problem to apply for a Hearing Dog.

"Many people mistakenly believe that they are not deaf enough to need a Hearing Dog, but I would say you have nothing to lose by applying. As soon as you start to lose self-confidence due to hearing loss, you find yourself on a fast-moving, downward spiral. Myrtle has helped me to recover from mine, and I owe her, and the wonderful staff at the Hearing Dog Center, an awful lot."

THERAPY DOGS

As the proud owner of a Pug, you will already know the joy that owning a dog can bring. Walks through the woods, cuddling on the sofa, and the companionship of sharing your emotions when you have had a bad or a great day – all these things enrich our lives. Imagine, then, what life would be like in the absence of your pet's company and unconditional love.

Many people live a life deprived of contact with animals. For lifelong animal lovers, living without a pet can be a great sadness. For example, many of the elderly in residential homes often find that the absence of animal companionship adds to their feelings of isolation and loneliness. In other cases, peoples' disabilities or circumstances have prevented them from ever experiencing the joy of dog ownership, such as the residents of children's homes or homes for the severely disabled. It is people such as these who benefit from regular contact with a therapy dog.

To become a therapy dog, your Pug will need to be character-assessed by one of the therapy dog organizations in your country. All therapy dogs must be totally trustworthy, and comfortable in unfamiliar surroundings and the company of strangers.

PUG BY NAME, PUG BY NATURE

Joan Corner has been involved with the Pets as Therapy (PAT) organization in the U.K. for nearly 20 years. Although she regularly visits a variety of establishments, Joan has achieved a great deal of success working with phobics, with her five-year-old Pug – aptly named Pug.

"My main breed has always been Bloodhounds, and I have done most of my therapy work with Bloodhounds. However, two years ago, a little three-year-old Pug came up for rehoming, and I couldn't resist him. I'd never owned a Pug before, and I couldn't think of a single name that was suitable, although I could think of plenty for Bloodhounds. So, in the end, I settled for the name Pug.

"Not long after I acquired Pug, I realized that he was suitable as a PAT dog. He passed his temperament test, his vaccinations were up to date, my references were suitable, and so we began visiting. PAT dogs need to be outgoing and responsive, gaining pleasure from a variety of human contact, and Pug was all of these. At first, he was a little shy, but he soon got into his stride, and now he loves it.

"Pug and I visit a variety of places, including residential homes and adult training centers, but I have found some of my most rewarding sessions have come from working with people who have phobias about dogs. It is wonderful to see the transformation in someone as their reactions change from abject terror to joy. I particularly remember one little boy whose life was turned around by Pug.

"Tom was completely and utterly petrified by dogs. When I first introduced him to Pug, it was from behind the safety of a large glass window – the extent of his fear was that bad. Gradually, Pug and Tom moved a little closer, until Tom was able to cope with Pug being in the same room. Within

Joan Corner and Pug have brought comfort and companionship to many.

another four sessions, Tom had progressed to the stage where he was confident enough to pet Pug, and, after that, there was no stopping them. They developed a strong bond, with Tom delighting in taking Pug for walks, petting him, and showing him to his family.

"I remember the first time Tom felt brave enough to take over walking Pug on a leash. It was really special. The hesitancy and fear completely vanished, replaced by pure pleasure and genuine happiness. Tom was so pleased that he ran up and down the corridor with Pug on the leash, and then dashed into the waiting room to show his mother and brother how well he had done. It was wonderful.

"Once he was confident with Pug, I introduced Tom to a series of larger dogs, and, eventually, to one of my Bloodhounds. Now he is working with a Rottweiler! The phobia that blighted his life is now well and truly under control, and a large part of that is due to Pug. Although Tom has stopped working with Pug, they remain friends and Tom is very attached. He brings gifts for Pug, sleeps with a picture of Pug above his bed, and has taken up a new hobby of sketching Pugs. It is wonderful to see such a dramatic change in a little boy who couldn't go near dogs before.

"Pug loves working as a therapy dog. Whenever we get ready to go to work, he becomes very excited. The attention, cuddles, and treats he receives give him a great deal of pleasure. For my part, I find it rewarding beyond words if I can bring a smile to an elderly person's day, or if I can change the life of someone who was previously so terrified of dogs that it affected every aspect of their daily lives.

"I've worked with several different breeds, and I think Pugs are ideally suited to therapy work – they appeal to people of all ages and backgrounds, and they have a wonderful temperament. Pug has truly shone as a therapy dog, and he is a credit to his breed."

PRIDE AND PREJUDICE

Breeder and exhibitor Alison Mount has a full-time job looking after her Pugs, but she still has time to get involved in therapy work. Alison concentrates on visiting the elderly, and here she describes some of her experiences.

"My therapy Pug is called Mr. Bennet, and he is six-and-a-half years old. I called him Mr. Bennet because, at the time, the BBC was showing a dramatization of Jane Austen's *Pride and Prejudice*, and it somehow seemed appropriate. Mr. Bennet's brother is called Mr. Darcy, while his sister is known as Lizzie.

"I work in residential homes for the elderly, and my job is to exercise and to communicate with the residents. That's how I got started.

When you talk to people on a daily basis, it is inevitable that they find out as much about you as you do about them, and Mr. Bennet frequently cropped up in the conversation. A few of the residents asked me to bring him in, so that they could see this wonderful dog I kept talking about, and it all took off from there.

"I have a very busy lifestyle, and I find that therapy work fits in really well. I visit two residential homes a week, as well as a daycare center occasionally. Each session takes about an hour, which doesn't seem very long, but it is amazing what you can achieve in that time. Both Mr. Bennet and I get a great deal of satisfaction from our visits.

"Mr. Bennet knows the days of the week we go visiting, and he gets very excited – he follows me around, as if to say 'Come on then, let's get going,' and he listens for the sound of me picking up my car keys. However, on the days of the week when we don't do therapy work, he couldn't care less! He really does love therapy work!

"It is extremely rewarding to see the effect that Mr. Bennet has on people. The residents love having a little dog to make a fuss over. Because Mr. Bennet is so small, he is easy to cuddle, and he loves climbing onto people's laps. I think he gives the residents the opportunity to become really affectionate with him without feeling foolish. He is also a great conversation starter. People seem to be more relaxed if there is a dog in the room demanding to be made a fuss over. Mr. Bennet is very popular wherever I take him, and he, of course, thrives on all the attention – not to mention the biscuits and ice cream!

"I've had quite a few memorable moments doing therapy work with Mr. Bennet. I remember one occasion when he visited an elderly gentleman called, oddly enough, Mr. Bennett. Even funnier was the fact that Mr. Bennett's son was also visiting, and his name was also – you guessed it – Mr. Bennett. So, we had three Mr. Bennetts in the room!

"One of my most moving experiences was when I was asked to take Mr. Bennet to the funeral of an elderly lady who had been particularly fond of him. The lady in question had been a very difficult lady to deal with, but she had adored Mr. Bennet. When the funeral arrangements were being made, the vicar (who

Mr. Bennet meets Mr. Bennett!

also visited the residential home) remembered an occasion when, at a Christmas party, this lady had fed Mr. Bennet five mince pies in a row. The vicar said he had never forgotten how much pleasure Mr. Bennet had given to this lady, and he later said so at her funeral service.

"After the funeral service had finished, everyone waited in their seats until Mr. Bennet and I began walking down the aisle to leave. Then they followed us out in a procession. This occurred not long after my mother had died, and her Labrador had also attended her funeral. The whole experience was very moving, and still affects me to this day.

"It can be a bit of an emotional roller coaster doing therapy work, as you can become very attached to people. However, there is also a great deal of fun to be had. Mr. Bennet loves attending parties, for example, and it is hilarious to see him sit at a table, eating sausage rolls and other treats, complete with party hat!

"I would tell anyone thinking of taking up pet therapy to go ahead and get involved. Get your dog assessed, take the tests, get going, and start bringing a little pleasure into someone's life."

CHAPTER NINE

SEEKING PERFECTION

There is something very special in owning a purebred dog – there is a sense of history and contributing to the continuation of a breed that, in the Pug's case, has survived millennia.

But what makes the Pug a Pug? Basically, he is recognizable because he conforms to a detailed set of characteristics – physical and temperamental – and these are outlined in a document called a Breed Standard.

Every breed has its own Standard, a written blueprint that describes all aspects of the perfect dog, including his coat, size, skeletal structure, and personality.

To ensure the Pug remains Puglike, and does not lose his unique characteristics over time, or at the hands of changing fashions in the show ring, breeders must produce dogs that are as close to the Standard as possible.

In the show ring, judges assess each entrant against the Standard. Those that are closest to the ideal are awarded places, and, if they are consistently successful, become Champions (see page 88). They then become sought after as breeding stock, and their genes and good qualities are passed on to the next generation. This way, breeders can strive for improvement of their breed, and ensure that the Pug becomes more healthy and handsome than ever.

THE BREED STANDARD

Every country's national kennel club has its own Breed Standard for the Pug. There may be some differences between countries, but, essentially, they are all fairly similar.

Here is a summary and explanation of the key points of the British and American Standards. For further details, contact your national kennel club for a copy of the Standard that specifically applies to you.

General appearance

A square-shaped dog, compact, and well

The Pug is a square-shaped, compact dog.

muscled – truly living up to the *multum in parvo* motto (see page 7).

Characteristics
Charming, dignified and intelligent – an ideal companion.

Temperament
The Pug has a stable, even temper. Happy, lively, playful, and outgoing, he exudes a real *joie de vivre*.

Head and skull
The head is large and round, with no indentation of the skull, and the muzzle is short. The top of the head is flat – it should not be domed like a Chihuahua's.

   The Pug's large, round head is a good example of neoteny – the retention of juvenile characteristics in an adult. The "baby" look is a popular feature of Toy breeds, where the dogs' sole function is to be companions that are loved and nurtured.

Eyes
The very large, round, globular eyes of the Pug again emphasize his "babyish" appeal. He has dark eyes and a soft expression, which becomes "full of fire" and passion when the dog is excited.

Ears
The Pug has never had to survive on his senses to hunt or avoid predators – he has relied purely on his good looks and loveable character. Therefore, he has never needed large or erect ears. Instead, his ears are small, thin, and silky soft – compared, in the KC and AKC Standards, to black velvet. As a companion dog, it is important that the ears are eminently strokable – something to which all Pug owners will attest!

The eyes give a soft expression.

Two types of ear are acceptable in the show ring: a rose ear and a button ear. With a rose ear, the ear leather is folded over and back. A button ear is preferred – this is where the flap folds forward, covering the inner ear, with the tip close to the head.

Mouth

Again, the Pug has never needed to rely on his mouth to carry quarry or rip up prey – his meals have always been provided for him! Therefore, his mouth has been developed purely with aesthetics in mind. He has a slightly undershot bite, meaning his bottom teeth marginally overlap the front teeth. He should not have a crooked mouth or show his teeth or tongue. The underjaw should be wide.

Neck

The neck is strong and thick, fitting in seamlessly with the "cobby" look of the body.

However, it is important that the Pug has sufficient length of neck to hold his head proudly.

Again, this is an aesthetic quality – not a practical one. In comparison, a functional breed such as the Greyhound would have a good reach of neck in order to hunt – in the Pug's case, all his key features are dictated by looks alone.

Forequarters

In keeping with his strong, muscular look, the Pug's straight legs are solid and powerful. Although he is a Toy breed, he has a strength and dignity that belies his size – even today, it is not difficult to imagine Pugs confidently trotting around the Imperial Palace in Beijing, as if they owned the place!

Body

The body is short and his chest wide, giving the dog his square appearance. He has a level topline, and a rounded rib cage. This provides plenty of room for the heart and lungs – important in a short-faced breed.

Hindquarters

Again, his legs are muscular and strong. His forelegs and hindlegs are all set well under the dog's body. This is in contrast to functional breeds, where the forelegs are placed forward and the hindlegs quite far back, thereby ensuring good reach and drive to cover large distances with power and speed. In the Pug's case, a solid trot is ample.

The Pug has a good turn of stifle (knee), meaning the hocks are well bent. Straight hocks often result in a bad topline.

Feet

Again, the feet do not need to do a lot of work, so they have been selectively bred for their looks alone. They should be medium-sized – not as long as a hare's foot, nor as round as a cat's. The toes are well split up – not too tight together, nor splayed. The nails are black, matching perfectly with the dog's dark markings. In the U.S., the dewclaws are removed – this is optional in the U.K.

Tail

The Pug's tail is known as the twist. It is set high on the body, and curls tightly over the hip bone. A double twist is especially desirable.

Gait/movement

When moving, the legs should be straight

A puppy tail, which is about to twist.

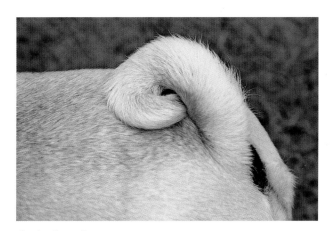

A single twist.

A double twist of the tail is highly desirable.

(when viewed from the front and the rear) and should reach well forward. The hindlegs move in a rolling gait. The ambling movement should be free, confident, and jaunty.

Coat

Black Pugs have a single topcoat, and lack the fluffy undercoat that the other colors enjoy. In all cases, the coat should be short and glossy, and consist of smooth, soft hair. As before, this makes the Pug a joy to stroke – therapy of the highest degree!

Color

The U.K. permits the following colors in the show ring: silver, apricot (a warm fawn), fawn, or black.

The U.S. permits three colors: silver, apricot-fawn, and black.

The color should be clearly contrasted with the trace (the black line that runs from the back of the dog's head to the base of the tail) and the dog's mask. Obviously, being whole-colored, this does not apply to black dogs. A trace is desirable, but often fades as the coat changes from puppyhood to adulthood, and many dogs do not have one.

The dog's markings should be black (the darker the better) and clearly defined. Markings include: the mask, ears, cheek moles, the thumbmark/diamond on the forehead, and the trace.

Size

The ideal weight for males and females is 14–18

The trace is a black line that runs from the back of the head to the base of the tail.

lbs (6.3–8.1 kg). This is a perfect weight for a companion dog, making him easy to pick up, and comfortable to have on your lap.

In reality, there are few dogs that fall within these weight limits in the show ring, as many dogs are being bred too large. Females are usually marginally smaller than the males, and should look feminine. Males should look masculine.

BREEDING

All purebred Pugs that are registered with a national kennel club have a pedigree – a piece of paper that gives the dog's family tree. If you are not familiar with pedigrees, they can initially look like a confusing sheet of names, but they are quite simple to follow.

The dog in question is on the far left of the pedigree, in a column all to himself. The next column features his parents – the father at the top and the mother at the bottom. This pattern is then replicated for all other generations, to grandparents, great-grandparents and so on.

If you study your dog's pedigree, you should be able to see what type of breeding is behind him – whether he was inbred, linebred, or outcrossed. Each breeding program has its own strengths and weaknesses.

Inbreeding

A mating in which two very close relatives are bred together, e.g. brother and sister, father and daughter, is called inbreeding. Inbreeding is used

Study your pug's pedigree so that you understand his bloodlines.

when the breeder wants to emphasize very quickly a particular trait associated with the family. However, as well as accentuating strengths, it can also replicate and exaggerate faults, so inbreeding should only be used by experienced breeders who have in-depth knowledge of the dogs' histories. Inbreeding is rarely done in the breed.

Linebreeding

This is the type favored by most breeders. It involves breeding more distant relations, those who share common ancestors, but are not directly related. Linebreeding is used to consolidate a line's features, without the high risk of doubling up on faults as can happen with inbreeding. Of course, the dogs should be selected carefully still, as hereditary problems can be replicated if unsuitable parents are used.

Outcrossing

This involves mating two totally unrelated dogs. Outcrossing is useful for injecting fresh blood into a line which can otherwise become "stale." Breeders usually outcross occasionally to bring in a certain characteristic and new genes. Out-crossing is useful to a line in the long term, and it is quite rare to produce a Champion from it in the first generation. However, with a careful eye, detailed research of breed lines, and a sprinkling of luck, it can be done.

The three pedigrees featured over the next few pages show Pug Champions that exemplify each type of breeding.

Inbreeding

Ch. Justabul Bartram (Bartie) wasn't planned – he was the result of an accidental mating when breeder Judith Boyes had arranged for friends to look after her dogs while she was away. Bartie's mother, Lily, saw her opportunity and managed to mate with a son from her first litter. Judith was not aware that the mating had taken place (had she known, she would have sought veterinary advice to prevent the pregnancy). By the time she realized it, it was too late to take action.

Judith kept all three puppies from the litter. Given the close breeding, she didn't want to sell the puppies in case health problems arose. Fortunately, there were no problems, and Bartie turned into a showstopper.

Ch. Justabul Bartram.

Parents	Grandparents	Great-Grandparents	Great-Great-Grandparents
Justabul Gerald	Ch. Master Edward Of Barryann	Adoram Rummage	Coljac Nikko Papas
			Calico of Adoram
		Eastonite Black Sue	Eastonite Hector
			Eastonite Tar Baby
	Bowcrest Estelle	Ch. Rexden Rubstic	Ansam Xavea
			Rexden Ramblyn Rose
		Sheafdon Comfrey of Bowcrest	Brukker Sargeant Tom
			Cuckoohaven Penelope of Sheafdon
Bowcrest Estelle	Ch. Rexden Rubstic	Ansam Xavea	Ch. Goodchance Eddystone
			Ansam Tammy
		Rexden Ramblyn Rose	It. Ch. Rexden Roughrider
			Tomarans Night Queen
	Sheafdon Comfrey	Brukker Sargeant Tom	Bluehopper of Bearland
			Cielos Sunshine
		Cuckoohaven Penelope of Sheafdon	Ch. Patrick of Paramin
			Candico of Cuckoohaven

Linebreeding

Ch. Hattella Fresh Parsley JW was born in August 1999, gained his first CC in September 2000, and became a Champion in April 2001, aged 20 months. To date, he has 17 CCs, was Top Puppy in 2002, Top Pug in 2001, Crufts Best of Breed winner in 2002 – going on to win second in the Toy Group.

This success is hardly surprising, considering that he comes from a good line of Champions. His father, and three of his four grandparents were all Champions, so breeder Carol Kirk was anxious to consolidate the best characteristics of her kennel type and used linebreeding to do it.

Ch. Hattella Fresh Parsley.

Parents	Grandparents	Great-Grandparents	Great-Great-Grandparents
Ch. Sheffawn Take That	Ch. Hattella Captain Dibble	Poosbury Piggy Malone	Pollywops Master Matthew at Telcontar
			Pallyn Pigtail of Poosbury
		Hattella Bella Dee	Ch. Hattella Wild Robin
			Cassandra Bella Donna
	Sheffawn Masquerade	Ch. Sheffawn Shannigan	Ch. Sylnor Fiery Emmett
			Sheffawn Rosie Dawn
		Sheffawn Merry Mandy	Hattella Much Morgan
			Greysuellas Pandora
Hattella See Jade	Ch. Ffain Devilline of Nanchyl	Ch. Nanchyl Zechim	Ch. Nanchyl Xerxes
			Ch. Nanchyl Venus
		Sheffawn Eastern Jewell	Ch. Sheffawn Shannigan
			Eastern Promise at Sheffawn
	Ch. Hattella See Coral	Poosbury Piggy Malone	Pollywops Master Matthew at Telcontar
			Pallyn Pigtail of Poosbury
		Hattella Bella Dee	Ch. Hattella Wild Robin
			Cassandra Bella Donna

Outcrossing

Breeder Sue Welch believes Ch. Skehana Highland Laddie was the best dog she ever bred. His dam, Skehana Rebecca, had done a fair bit of winning, and his father was a Champion – Ardglass Benjamin. Sue saw Benjamin at shows and knew he would suit Rebecca, so she travelled hundreds of miles to Scotland to mate the two.

Fortunately, the journey was not in vain. Laddie won a reserve CC at the age of just seven months, and became a Champion at two-and-a-half years.

Laddie produced two Champions: Ch. Skehana Hanah and Ch. Skehana Jacqueline. His litter sister, Ch. Heather of Ardglass, also became a champion.

Ch. Skehana Highland Laddie.

Parents	Grandparents	Great-Grandparents	Great-Great-Grandparents
Ch. Ardglass Benjamin	Ch. Nanchyl Zechim	Champion Nanchyl Xerxes	Nanchyl Nimbus
			Ch. Nanchyl Roxanna
		Ch. Nanchyl Venus	Ch. Slepe Kerrygold
			Ch. Nanchyl Ophelia
	Ardglass Phyliss	Ardglass Guy Fawkes	Pugnus Caesar of Ardglass
			Ardglass Isadora
		Ardglass Faith	Ch. Ardglass Sorlion
			Ardglass Tina
Skehana Rebecca	Ch. Harjen Merry Porthos of Adoram	Ch. Ansam Dantie	Ch. Eastonite Arthur of Elmsleigh
			Ansam Tammy
		Paramin Phoenix	Paramin Paul
			Yung Lu Lu Fu
	Skehana Shady Lady	Ch. Pyenest Nicholas	Ansam Xavea
			Pyenest Zoe Darling
		Skehana Silver Queen	Verwood Quail of Skehana
			Silver Belle of Skehana

PUPPY TO CHAMPION

All puppies are individual and mature at a different rate. The usual development is that the markings become darker, the twist (tail) curls up, and the dog bulks out in the body – particularly around the neck and chest. There are no hard-and-fast rules about when these changes occur. For example, the twist can curl as early as eight weeks or as late six months.

These photos show how Ch. Jansara Daniella (Danni) developed from puppy to Champion. Danni is a show girl in a million. Owner and breeder Sarah Hayward bred a litter and the only female produced was Danni, whom she kept for her breeding line. However, Danni was quite a nervous puppy, and Sarah offered her to someone else – who turned her down. Fortunately, Danni blossomed and has become a legend in the breed.

Notable successes include winning Best in Show at Windsor Championship Show in 1999, Best in Show at U.K. Toy Dogs 1999, and three Reserve Best in Shows at other Championship Shows. Danni has won six Toy Groups, was Best of Breed at Crufts 2000, and in 1999 was the eighth top-winning dog of all breeds. She was Top Pug in 1999 and 2000.

Danni matured quite early, as the photos show. Sarah started showing Danni when she was six months old, by which time she was already like a mature adult (some Pugs can take up to two years to mature properly). She was crowned a Champion at the age of two-and-a-half years, having won three Challenge Certificates in just three weeks! In total, she has notched up an impressive tally of 17 CCs in her career.

Danni, age 10 weeks.

Age 13 months.

Ch. Jansara Daniella, at 4 years old, winner of 17 CCs.

CHAPTER TEN

HEALTH CARE

The Pug, a Mastiff in miniature, has a long history of domestication during which his size may have reduced but not his robust physique and natural hardiness! More substantial than the majority of his companions in the Toy Group, he is really a very hardy companion dog with surprisingly few breed-associated problems. Certainly, his flattened (brachycephalic) face can occasionally lead to certain airway obstruction problems and his reputation for snoring is legendary. Nevertheless he is, on the whole, a very healthy little dog.

First, we begin with the important subject of preventative care, then general first-aid principles will be explored, and finally breed-prone problems will be discussed.

PREVENTIVE CARE

There is much more to preventive care than simply vaccination and worming. Responsible preventive care involves:

- A vaccination program tailored to suit the needs of your dog, your lifestyle, and environment.
- Comprehensive parasite control.
- Adequate appropriate exercise. Pugs are stocky little dogs prone to run to fat at an early age if not adequately exercised. Conversely, too much exercise at too young an age can result in certain joint and bone problems.
- Grooming – the Breed Standard calls for a fine, smooth, soft, short, and glossy coat. Brushing and combing is minimal but should not be ignored. Grooming includes regular attention to ears, eyes, and teeth (page 58) to avoid future problems.
- Training – Pugs are intelligent and relatively easy to train. Start as soon as you acquire the puppy, training by reward rather than by punishment, and you will find that your Pug will thrive on the experience (chapter four).
- Once vaccinations are completed and your puppy is free to mix, enroll with a local training

Natural immunity is topped up by antibodies absorbed from the milk when suckling.

club. The effort is well worthwhile, resulting in a well-integrated companion who knows how to behave in the presence of his peers and realizes that you are the symbolic pack leader, whose merest gesture must be obeyed and never challenged for any reason. This is time well spent. The transition to training classes can be made even easier by enrolling for puppy socialization classes if they are available at a location near you.

VACCINATION

Vaccination or inoculation (throughout this chapter, the terms will be used synonymously), stimulates the dog to produce active immunity against one or more diseases, without actually developing any symptoms of that disease. This is despite the fact that the causative organism has been introduced into the dog. This is effectively achieved by altering the bacteria or viruses (pathogens) that are responsible for the disease, but at the same time ensuring that any alteration does not interfere with the host's ability to recognize it as a threat and build up resistance – antibodies. The pathogens can either be killed (inactivated) or weakened (attenuated).

Once altered, the appropriate pathogens can be introduced into the body by various routes. Vaccination against kennel cough (infectious bronchotracheitis), for example, is by administering nasal drops. Inoculations generally involve injections, perhaps one of the reasons that in the U.K. these are so often referred to as "jabs."

Irrespective of whether an inactivated or an attenuated vaccine is used, the body produces an active immunity. This lasts a variable time, depending on the vaccine used, the disease, and the age and health of the dog.

Discuss booster requirements with your veterinarian.

NATURAL IMMUNITY

Puppies are usually born with some immunity that is acquired from their mother while still in the womb. The necessary antibodies are carried in the blood, and cross the placenta into the puppy. This is acquired (passive) immunity. It only lasts for about three weeks if not regularly topped up via antibodies absorbed from the milk when suckling.

Passive protection starts to wane once weaning begins. It disappears about a month after the puppy has left his mother. This is the correct time to start vaccinations. It is also the danger period for the puppy, since, at this time, he is susceptible to any naturally acquired infection. It is for this reason that you are asked to isolate your Pug puppy for 10 to 14 days after completion of inoculation while the puppy develops active immunity to the vaccine. During this period, the puppy is not protected.

One of the main aims of vaccine manufacturers is to develop vaccines that will confer solid protection in the shortest possible time, even when circulating maternal antibodies are present. Canine vaccines are available that can be completed by 10 to 12 weeks of age. This affords your puppy early immunity and allows early socialization and training.

SAFE SOCIALIZATION

Allow your new puppy a day or two to settle into the new surroundings, then call your veterinarian. Inquire about vaccinations, costs, appointment details, and clinic facilities (see page 25), and, at the same time, ask about puppy classes. These socialization classes are good fun and lay the foundations of canine etiquette. They allow a degree of controlled interaction between puppies of all ages and breeds. Although the puppies are often not fully vaccinated, they will all have undergone a veterinary examination.

BOOSTING

Vaccination does not give lifelong immunity; reinforcement (boosting) will be required. Killed vaccines generally require more frequent boosting, usually annually (although sometimes even less often).

Manufacturers have produced multivalent canine vaccines that cover several diseases with one injection. However, when short-acting (usually inactivated) components are incorporated into the multidisease shot, reinoculation of the product as a whole is based on the component that gives the shortest protection. Thus, although effective protection against distemper and hepatitis will last much longer than a year, because this is combined with leptospirosis, the manufacturer's recommendation will be that an annual booster of the combined vaccine is advised.

VACCINATION REACTIONS

Until relatively recently, vaccination recommendations were manufacturer-led. However, in response to owners' concerns regarding possible vaccination reactions, things are beginning to change.

Primary vaccination and boosters are now tailored for individual requirements. Discuss this with your veterinarian at the time of the primary vaccination.

In a very small number of cases, there is evidence that vaccination can result in untoward reactions. These usually involve the immune system and result in problems such as anemia. Vaccine safety involves risks and benefits. I think risk exists, but the risk of reemergence of these killer diseases is much greater if we allow our pets' immune status to fall dangerously. What can be done?

Your dog's immunity to a variety of diseases can be determined from a small blood sample that will indicate whether boosting is required for any particular disease. Cost-wise, this will be considerably more expensive than a combined booster injection and there is also the question of stress for the dog. Pugs are stoic, but stress levels at having to undergo venipuncture (injection into the vein) will be considerably greater than a simple shot.

Discuss your concerns with your veterinarian to help you reach an informed decision.

CORE AND NONCORE VACCINES

Core vaccines are the necessary ones that protect against diseases that are serious, fatal, or difficult to treat. In Britain, these include distemper, parvovirus, and hepatitis (adenovirus) disease. In North America, rabies is also a core vaccine. In the U.K., this is also true if you intend to visit any of the countries in the "PETS" travel scheme. This allows entry into Britain without having to undergo the mandatory six months quarantine.

Noncore vaccines include bordetella (kennel cough) and leptospirosis (kidney disease). In the U.S., other diseases, such as coronavirus, which causes diarrhea, and borellia (Lyme disease), which causes infective polyarthritis, are also included.

Which noncore vaccines are used depends upon a risk assessment with your veterinarian.

The general consensus is that primary inoculation and the first annual booster, when the dog is about 15 months of age, are sound preventive medicine. These vaccines should include the core vaccines and those noncore vaccines considered appropriate. Future vaccinations will then depend upon other factors, including local infection levels, breed susceptibilities, lifestyle (e.g. whether you go to shows, training classes, boarding kennels, and so forth).

CANINE DISTEMPER

Canine distemper is no longer widespread in most developed Western countries, solely due to vaccination.

Signs (symptoms) include fever, diarrhea, coughing, with discharges from the nose and eyes. With the "hardpad" variant, the pads can harden. A significant proportion of infected dogs develop nervous signs, including fits, chorea (muscle-twitching), and paralysis.

Due to vaccination, distemper is hardly ever seen in pet dogs today – but do not be misled! The virus is still out there, waiting for its opportunity. This was demonstrated in Finland only a few years ago when a serious epidemic of distemper occurred solely due to falling levels of immunity in the canine population.

HEPATITIS

This is also known as adenovirus disease. Signs range from sudden death in very acute infection, to mild cases where the dog only appears to be a bit "off-color." In severe cases, there is usually fever, enlargement of all the lymph nodes (glands), and a swollen liver. Sometimes "blue eye" can occur, where one or both eyes looks opaque and bluish, due to swelling of the cornea

Vaccination against rabies is compulsory in many countries.

(clear part of the eye). Thankfully, the condition usually resolves quickly without problems.

PARVOVIRUS

This virus is very stable and can exist in the environment for a long time. The disease reached epidemic proportions in Europe and North America in the 1980s. Signs include vomiting and blood-stained diarrhea (dysentery). The rapid development of safe, effective vaccines brought the disease under control in the Western world, although it is still a serious killer, rivalling only distemper in many other countries.

RABIES

Rabies vaccination is compulsory in many countries, including the United States. In Britain, it is mandatory for dogs traveling under the PETS scheme. The virus is spread by bites from infected animals. These include foxes in Europe, and stray dogs in other parts of the world.

KENNEL COUGH

In North America, parainfluenza is considered to be the primary cause of the kennel cough syndrome, (infectious bronchotracheitis); in Britain, *Bordetella bronchiseptica*, a bacterium, is considered the culprit.

Irrespective of the cause, the disease is not usually life-threatening except in very young and very old dogs. A persistent cough for three to four weeks is the main symptom, which results in rapid spread of the disease.

A parainfluenza component has been

Kennel cough spreads quickly when dogs are housed together.

incorporated in multivalent vaccines for some years. The manufacturers recommend annual revaccination with the suggestion that, in high-risk situations, e.g. boarding kennels, shows, and so forth, even more frequent revaccination should be considered.

Unlike parainfluenza, bordetella is not incorporated into the usual multivalent vaccines since it is usually administered separately via nasal drops. These have been shown to give better immunity than conventional inoculation. In Britain, there is a combined parainfluenza and bordetella intranasal vaccine available.

If you do normally go to dog shows, training classes, or regularly board your Pug, think about protection against bordetellosis and parainfluenza. Along with Boxers, Bulldogs, and many other breeds, Pugs are brachycephalic. Their short faces make breathing difficult if they have any upper respiratory tract infection. Prevention is better than cure!

LEPTOSPIROSIS

Leptospirosis is caused by bacteria and not by viruses. Protection against two diseases is provided by the killed (inactivated) leptospirosis vaccine.

Leptospira canicola is spread mainly in the urine of infected dogs. Another form, *Leptospira icterohaemorrhagiae* is spread by rats. Both types cause disease in dogs and can spread to humans.

Recent work has shown that dogs infected with leptospirosis in the U.K. are usually infected with other types. Since *L. icterohaemorrhagiae* causes Weil's disease in humans and *L. canicola*

can also affect us, these are the reasons for the present vaccination policy. The leptospiral vaccine is probably the shortest-acting of all the various components in multivalent vaccines.

CANINE CORONAVIRUS

This virus can cause diarrhea, particularly in puppies. The disease is usually mild and responds to supportive therapy. A vaccine is available in North America and some European countries, but no licensed vaccine is currently available in Britain.

LYME DISEASE

This disease, caused by a bacterial spirochaete, is carried by certain ticks whose bite can transmit the disease to dogs and humans. It is very common in parts of North America and it does occur in the U.K. It causes acute polyarthritis in both dogs and people. Fever, heart, kidney, and neurological problems can also occur.

Although vaccines are available in North America, there is currently no licensed vaccine available in Britain.

PARASITES

Parasite control is an important part of preventative healthcare and is essential for all dogs, irrespective of size or lifestyle. Parasites are roughly divided into two groups:

- **Ectoparasites** live on the surface of the host, and include fleas, lice, ticks, and mites.
- **Endoparasites** live within the host. Worms are the most well known, but there are other

important endoparasites, such as Coccidia and Giardia, although these may not be quite so widespread.

FLEAS

Fleas are the most common ectoparasites found on dogs. Pugs, although classified as Toy dogs, are sociable, hardy individuals, happy to be outside, and can pick fleas up from the environment or from contact with other animals.

Some dogs will carry a very high flea burden without problems, whereas others will show evidence of typical flea allergy dermatitis (FAD). Although FAD is not common, it does affect the Pug. Once hypersensitivity occurs, all that is

The dog flea – Ctenocephalides canis

needed is a bite from one flea to start the serious pruritis (itching). Sometimes, no fleas can be found on the dog, although there is usually evidence of flea dirt. Always check for this when grooming.

Fleas are not host-specific. Cat and raccoon fleas can affect dogs, and all types of fleas can bite humans as well as a range of other animals.

Life Cycle

Effective control involves both adult fleas on the dog and also the immature stages that develop in the home. Fleas need a meal of blood to complete their life cycle. The adult flea then lays eggs on the dog. These soon drop to the ground. Provided that the temperature and humidity are within the correct range, they develop into larvae (immature forms) in carpets or gaps between floorboards.

Development can also take place outdoors, provided conditions are suitable. Many pet dogs (and cats) have areas in even the tiniest yards where they like to lie. Such areas can be difficult to render flea-free!

Under ideal conditions, the life cycle can be completed in only three weeks. Sometimes, fleas can live without feeding for more than a year. This is why dogs and people can be bitten when entering a property that has been left totally unoccupied for some time.

Flea Control

Adult fleas account for only approximately 5 percent of the total flea population. Control of the other 95 percent, consisting of immature stages, can be much more difficult. Few environmental insecticides have any effect against immature fleas, so an insecticide with prolonged action should be used. This will be effective against any subsequently emerging adults. Control in the home should also involve thorough vacuuming to remove any flea larvae.

Oral preparations are also available, which, given to your dog, will prevent the completion

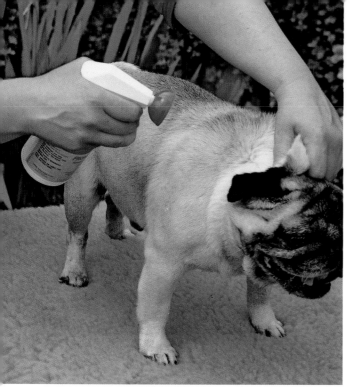

When the flea bites your Pug to get its blood meal, it has to penetrate the fat layer to get to the blood supply, and so ingests the chemical. If the dog gets wet or is bathed occasionally, the efficacy of the treatment is not affected. It is important to reapply the preparation according to the manufacturers' recommendation. This is usually every 30 or 60 days depending on the product.

Some preparations are also effective against certain endoparasites particularly roundworms. These are called endectocides.

LICE

Lice do not appear to be a problem in Pugs except occasionally in puppy farm (puppy mill) animals.

Lice require direct contact for transmission, and, unlike fleas, the whole life cycle occurs on the host. The eggs (nits) are attached to individual hairs. Infestation is usually associated with violent itching, and often affects the head and ears. Unlike fleas, lice can be controlled by bathing in an effective ectoparasite shampoo.

TICKS

Ticks are carriers of various diseases – Lyme disease (borelliosis), babesiosis, and ehrlichiosis are examples. Although these diseases have been recognized in the U.K., they are more common in warmer parts of Europe and the United States.

Several flea and lice preparations are effective for tick control. Your veterinarian will advise on the best choice.

It is essential to control flea infestation.

of the life cycle of the fleas. The compound is transferred to the adult flea when it bites the dog for the all-essential blood meal.

There are many effective preparations to control adult fleas on the dog. Sprays can be used, but most dogs dislike the noise, and care must be taken to avoid the eyes.

Insecticidal baths are useful for killing adult fleas in the coat, but they do not have a lasting effect. Bathing should always be combined with other methods of flea control to reduce rapid reinfestation.

Prolonged-action on-the-spot preparations are very effective and easy to use on a Pug. These preparations contain a chemical that is lethal to the flea. It is dissolved in a medium that spreads through the invisible fat layer on the skin. Within 24 hours, the dog has total protection against fleas for approximately two months.

Dogs that live in the country are more likely to pick up ticks.

CHEYLETIELLOSIS

Cheyletiella yasguri, the causal mite, can just be seen by the naked eye as a tiny white speck, hence the term "walking dandruff." Young Pugs that appear itchy and scurfy, particularly along the back, are prime suspects. The mite is zoonotic (can affect humans) and can cause intense irritation, particularly in children.

Sprays, bathing, and on-the-spot preparations are all effective. Other pets should be treated to ensure that re-infestation does not recur. Veterinary advice is worthwhile.

HARVEST MITES

These are the larvae (immature forms) of a mite that lives in decaying organic matter. They are red, and just visible to the naked eye. Pugs, particularly if exercised in fields and woodlands with a chalky soil, can be susceptible to harvest mites. Generally, it is the muzzle, head, and feet that are affected.

Any of the usual insecticidal sprays or washes are effective, but reapplication is necessary if you live in an area where this larval mite is common.

MANGE

Mange is a parasitic skin disease caused by microscopic mites, two of which are a problem in dogs, causing demodectic and sarcoptic mange. Both are uncommon in the Pug, although the breed is said to be prone to demodex.

DEMODECTIC MANGE

Demodex mites live in the hair follicles and sebaceous glands of many normal dogs. They only cause problems if the host becomes immuno-incompetent for any reason. It is for this reason that demodectic mange is not thought of as a contagious disease in the same way as sarcoptic mange.

If the demodex mite starts to multiply, signs (including inflammation and hair loss) are seen. Itching is often minimal but secondary bacterial infection can be a problem.

Veterinary treatment using modern preparations is generally effective once a positive diagnosis has been made.

SARCOPTIC MANGE

Sarcoptic mange is zoonotic. It causes scabies, which is intensely pruritic (itchy), and children are particularly susceptible. Itchy areas develop on the arms and abdomen as a result of nursing the affected animal.

Modern veterinary treatments are effective,

All puppies carry a burden of roundworm

but depend on accurate diagnosis which sometimes requires repeated skin scrapings. Consult your veterinarian if you suspect this condition.

ENDOPARASITES

Intestinal worms are by far the most important endoparasites in the dog. Protozoan parasites such as Coccidia and Giardia may also be a problem in certain areas, particularly in North America.

ROUNDWORMS

Until relatively recently, all puppies were considered to have worms. Understanding of the complex life cycle, together with the development of more effective roundworm remedies, have resulted in a dramatic reduction in the number of worm-infested dogs and puppies.

The most common roundworm is *Toxocara canis*. This is a large, round, white worm 3–6 in.

(7–15 cm) long. The life cycle is complex. Puppies can be born with toxocariasis acquired from their mother before birth. Regular worming of puppies and adults is essential.

Roundworm larvae can remain dormant in the tissues of adult dogs indefinitely. In the female, under the influence of hormones during pregnancy, they become activated, cross the placenta into the bloodstream, and enter the puppy. They finally develop into adult worms in the small intestine. Larvae can also be passed from the female to the puppy during suckling.

There are now many safe and effective worm treatments available. Endecticides are on-the-spot preparations similar to those used for flea control. They contain drugs (e.g. selamectin) which are highly effective not only against fleas but also roundworms and heartworms. Endectocides can be useful if you have difficulty administering oral preparations.

There are preparations licensed for use in

puppies from 14 days of age. Some preparations are available over the counter, but veterinary advice is recommended to establish an effective lifelong worming strategy.

There is a slight risk of roundworms being transmitted to humans. For this reason, veterinarians advise that all adult dogs are routinely wormed approximately twice a year.

TAPEWORMS

This is the other common type of intestinal worm found in the dog. Unlike roundworms, they do not have a direct life cycle, so spread is

The flat face of the Pug can result in breathing problems.

not from dog to dog but through an intermediate host. The host varies according to the type of tapeworm, and include fleas, sheep, horses, rodents, and sometimes even humans!

In the dog, the most common type of tapeworm is *Dipylidium caninum*. This worm, which can be up to 20 in. (50 cm), uses the flea as the intermediate host. The worms live in the intestine. Eggs contained within mature segments are shed from the end of the worm, and pass out in the dog's feces. These segments are sticky and look like small grains of rice. In infested dogs, they can often be seen around the anus. The segments finally fall to the ground, dry, and burst, releasing the microscopic eggs.

Free-living flea larvae eat these eggs, which develop as the flea matures. When the adult flea is swallowed by a susceptible dog, the life cycle of the tapeworm is completed.

Effective treatment involves both the tapeworm and the eradication of fleas in the environment. Enlist the help of your veterinarian.

Other tapeworms can be a problem in dogs that regularly eat the meat of intermediate hosts, such as rabbits, hares, and similar wildlife. Echinococcus species deserve mention since they have a zoonotic potential. *Echinococcus multilocularis* can cause serious cysts in the lungs of people. In the U.K., under the PETS scheme, dogs and cats have to be treated with specific remedies against this cestode (and so certified) before entry or reentry is allowed. This should be kept in mind by anyone who intends to travel to any of the PETS-authorized countries from Britain with a dog.

HEARTWORM

Dirofilaria immitis causes major problems in many of the warmer parts of the world, including North America. Selamectin (mentioned previously) is one of the effective drugs available. Consult your veterinarian if heartworm is a problem in your area.

OTHER INTESTINAL WORMS

Hookworms (*Uncinaria* and *Ancylostoma* species), together with whipworms (*Trichuris vulpis*), are occasionally the cause of poor general condition in dogs.

More severe signs, such as anemia or dysentery, can occur. These worms are usually associated with kennel dogs in the U.K. They are often discovered during routine fecal investigation rather than because of illness. Treatment is uncomplicated with modern preparations from your veterinarian.

GIARDIA AND COCCIDIA

These microscopic protozoan endoparasites can cause diarrhea problems, particularly in puppies. Giardia is a waterborne disease, more common in North America than in Britain. The disease can occur in the U.K. in imported dogs. This is likely to increase with the relaxation of quarantine regulations.

Giardiasis is considered to be zoonotic, and is the most common intestinal parasite in humans in America. Nevertheless, there is no conclusive evidence that cysts shed by dogs (and cats) are infective to humans.

If you are concerned, a simple stool test can be carried out by your veterinarian.

EMERGENCY CARE AND FIRST AID

Pugs are really big dogs in little bodies. They tend to be into everything and so all sorts of emergencies can occur – bites, burns, broken legs, heatstroke, insect stings, and poisoning are just a few. All occur without warning, otherwise they would not be emergencies!

First aid is the initial treatment given in any emergency. The purpose is to preserve life, reduce pain and discomfort, minimize the risk of permanent disability or disfigurement, and to prevent further injury.

EMERGENCY PROCEDURES

Regardless of the cause, in any emergency there is a certain protocol that is worth observing:

- Keep calm and do not panic.
- Get help, if possible.
- Contact your veterinarian, explain the situation, and obtain specific advice.
- If there is possible internal injury, try to keep the patient as still as possible. With a dog the size of a Pug, a cardboard box or other makeshift container is a good idea, but make sure that he cannot injure himself further by jumping out.
- Use the box to convey your pet to the veterinarian as soon as possible.
- Drive carefully and observe the speed limits.

Depending on the nature of the emergency, it may be necessary to carry out first aid on site. You will find that following a sequential routine – the A, B, C of first aid – will help.

A is for Airway. This means checking the mouth and throat, and ensuring that there is no obstruction preventing air from reaching the lungs.

B is for Breathing. Check to see if there are signs of breathing.

C is for Collapse. Make sure the heart is beating.

How does this system work? Imagine a dog choking because there is something lodged in his mouth or throat. A is for Airway: Endeavor to remove any blockage first. Take care! Remember that the most docile, affectionate pet in such a situation is terrified. Try to avoid getting bitten. Use a stick or other blunt implement to gently dislodge anything in the mouth. Wrap tissues around the instrument to remove any vomit, saliva, or other matter.

Once the airway is clear, go to B, and check for Breathing. Place the palm of your hand around the chest, just behind the forelegs. Can you feel a heartbeat? Is the chest moving? This will also combine C for Collapse, which also covers circulation.

If there is no movement of the ribs and you can feel no heartbeat (pulse), artificial respiration and cardiac massage can be easily combined in a dog the size of a Pug. The heart is situated in the lower part of the chest, just at the level of the elbows. Place your hand around the sternum, fingers on one side and the thumb on the other. Use both hands if that is more comfortable. Start gently squeezing approximately 20 to 25 times a minute. This has the dual function of stimulating the heart and helping to get

Urgent attention is required if a dog goes into shock.

air into the lungs. After about every 10 squeezes, check for a heartbeat and breathing. If you manage to start the heart, continue for several minutes. This is cardiopulmonary resuscitation (CPR).

Check the color of the mucous membranes of the gums or under the lips. When you first started, this area was probably white or ashen gray. Once the heart is beating, a vague pink tinge should return. This return of color will be very subtle because your dog will be in shock.

SHOCK

Shock is a complex condition disrupting the delicate fluid balance of the body. It is always accompanied by a serious fall in blood pressure. Causes include serious hemorrhage, heart failure, heatstroke, and acute allergic reactions. Signs of shock can include:

- Rapid breathing
- Rapid heart rate
- Pallor of the mucous membranes of the gums, lips, and under the eyelids
- Severe depression
- A cold feel to the limbs and ears
- Sometimes vomiting.

The most important first-aid treatment for shock is to keep the dog warm. Do not apply too much external heat – instead wrap him in blankets, newspapers, clothes, whatever is available, and get him to your veterinarian as soon as possible.

Here is a brief outline of first aid procedures for some of the common emergencies that can occur with your Pug. The list is by no means comprehensive but knowledge of how to deal with these conditions should help when confronted with any emergency.

BLEEDING

Torn claws will normally result in quite severe hemorrhage in Pugs. Bleeding from the limbs should be bandaged fairly tightly, using a clean bandage or any clean material. A polyethylene bag in an emergency can then be bandaged on to the limb to prevent further blood loss.

Bleeding from other parts of the body including the head or ears cannot be so easily controlled. In these cases, try applying a cold compress, and finger- or hand-pressure to stem the flow.

BURNS AND SCALDS

Cool the burned or scalded area with cold water as quickly as possible. If it is due to a caustic substance, such as drain cleaner or bleach, wash away as much as you can with plenty of cold water. Even if there does not appear too much cause for concern, get to your veterinarian as soon as you can. This will often avoid sloughing off the burned/scalded area a few days later.

EYE INJURIES

Pugs are renowned for their large, expressive eyes – but they can be vulnerable. Scratches from bushes and cats' claws are common injuries. Cold water, or, better still, saline solution (contact lens solution), liberally applied with a pad should be used to cleanse the eye. If the eyeball appears to be injured or if there is any bleeding, try to cover it with a pad soaked in cold water, and get to your veterinarian as soon as possible.

HEATSTROKE

Because of their flat-faced (brachycephalic) shape, Pugs can be susceptible to heatstroke. In warm, humid weather, this can occur rapidly. Conservatories and poorly ventilated rooms can be just as dangerous as cars. Your Pug doesn't necessarily need to be in the sun for the condition to strike.

First signs are excessive panting with obvious breathing distress (stertor). Coma and death can quickly follow, due to irreversible changes in the blood vessels. Reduce the temperature as quickly as possible. Plunge or bathe the dog in cold

Spraying with cool water on a hot day is a good way of reducing body temperature.

water. Place ice on the gums, under the tail, and in the groin. Then take the still-wet animal to the veterinarian as soon as possible.

FITS AND SEIZURES

During a fit (seizure), your Pug is unconscious and oblivious. Nevertheless, it is pretty terrifying for onlookers. Prevent injury while the dog is thrashing about. A cardboard box is useful. Immediately after the seizure, the dog is unlikely to be able to see, hear, or feel properly, and therefore will be less likely to frighten or injure himself if suitably confined. Subdued light will hasten recovery. Most seizures only last a few seconds or minutes but it will seem an eternity to you.

If still seizuring after a few minutes, telephone your veterinarian for advice. Otherwise, once past the fit and fairly conscious, take him to your veterinarian, still in the container, if possible.

BREED-PRONE PROBLEMS

Think of the Pug as a solidly constructed Mastiff in miniature, and it is hardly surprising that specific breed problems are few. Those that occur are either shared by other members of the Toy Group or are conformation-related. For example, brachycephalic airway obstruction syndrome (BAOS) does occur. This is related to the flattened face and results in breathing problems. Slipping kneecaps, shared with many members of the Toy Group, also occur.

Black Pugs have a single topcoat.

BRACHYCEPHALIC AIRWAY OBSTRUCTION SYNDROME (BAOS)

This affects many flat-faced breeds – English Bulldogs, Pekingese, and Pugs among them. The usual signs are exercise intolerance even in a relatively young dog, and noisy or difficult breathing.

Pugs of any age can be affected, and the condition is exacerbated by obesity, hot weather, exercise, and excitement. In severe cases, the Pug may collapse and display blue mucous membranes (cyanosis).

Dogs with brachycephalic conformation have difficulty filling the lungs. This in turn may result in the swelling of the nasal passages and throat (airway edema), which further reduces air flow. Thus a vicious cycle supervenes. The impeded air flow prevents adequate heat loss through panting so, particularly in hot weather, hyperthermia (heatstroke) can occur (see page 124).

There are several causes. The most common in Pugs is an elongated soft palate, which may overlay the larynx and prevent air getting to the lungs. Stenotic nares (small nostrils) are another common problem, or there can be problems with the larynx, thus preventing adequate air intake.

Treatment involves cooling the patient if hyperthermic (see page 124), and surgical correction of the anatomical defect if feasible.

In many cases, the condition has a congenital origin and therefore it is wise not to breed from any affected individuals.

The Pug is a healthy breed, but owners should be aware of inherited disorders that can occur.

ORTHOPEDIC PROBLEMS

Hemivertebrae

Butterfly vertebrae or other improperly formed vertebrae occur in Pugs occasionally. Sometimes, the condition only comes to light when the dog is X-rayed for other reasons. Lameness or pain along the spine may be evident. If concerned, veterinary advice should be sought.

Luxating Patella

Slipping kneecaps (luxating patellae) are basically joint problems. The kneecap moves in a groove at the lower end of the femur (thigh bone). Some dogs are born with a groove that is not deep enough to retain the kneecap, so that it will "pop out" of the groove, usually to the inside of the joint (medial patella luxation). This causes the dog to hop for a few steps. If mildly affected, the kneecap will often return to its groove and the signs disappear.

Sometimes both legs are affected, and, particularly if your Pug is overweight, the condition can be crippling.

Often the condition first becomes noticeable when the puppy is only a few months old. Every so often, the dog appears to hop on one of the hindlegs.

There are very successful surgical techniques available to correct the problem. It is wise to refrain from breeding from any affected individuals.

The Pug's prominent eyes can be vulnerable to injury.

Elbow Dislocation

This is another congenital developmental abnormality. Usually the only signs are lameness although, occasionally, the foreleg may appear severely deformed at the elbow. Although relatively rare, there is a preponderance in brachycephalic breeds. Provided the condition is diagnosed early enough, successful surgical repair is possible but, of course, it is then unwise to use the dog for breeding.

DENTAL PROBLEMS

Like many Toy dogs, Pugs do suffer dental problems at an earlier age than one would expect. In the Pug, much can be done to reduce the problem if regular home care procedures are adopted from an early age. There are many special chews, foods, and toys available to delay dental problems, but home brushing with a suitable canine dentifrice is by far the most effective prophylactic. Discuss this with your veterinarian at the time primary vaccinations are carried out. The earlier that

procedures are put into place, the easier it is for your Pug to accept them as part of the regular routine (see page 62).

EYE CONDITIONS

Breed Standards for Pugs call for a very large, slightly prominent eye. Such conformation can predispose the breed to certain eye problems. Apart from their vulnerability to injury, Pugs' eyes can cause problems due to keratoconjunctivitis sicca (KCS or dry eye) which can be due to lack of formation of sufficient tears, or to the drying-out of the surface of the eye.

A condition called pigmentary keratitis can also occur, which is a deposit of black pigment (melanin) in the cornea. Both conditions occur in many brachycephalic, prominent-eyed, breeds. Entropion (inturning of the eyelids) may also cause irritation.

Although these conditions may involve referral to a specialist veterinary ophthalmologist, there are effective treatments available.

With good care and management, your Pug should live a long and healthy life.

HEART PROBLEMS

Many brachycephalic breeds have heart problems, and it is my experience that the Pug is probably among the least affected of all the flat-faced breeds. Often, heart problems are suspected when the basic condition is BAOS (see page 125). Congenital heart problems do occur, however.

The usual signs are exercise intolerance and shortness of breath, even in very young dogs. If you have concerns, a cardiac checkup from your veterinarian makes good sense.

SUMMARY

Essentially, the Pug is a healthy, robust breed, despite his small size, who will provide many years of companionship and happiness, as long as his basic needs are furnished and he receives good care and management.